SECOND CLASS

How the Elites Betrayed America's
— Working Men and Women —

BATYA UNGAR-SARGON

Encounter
BOOKS

New York • London

First American edition published in 2024 by Encounter Books,
an activity of Encounter for Culture and Education, Inc.,
a nonprofit, tax-exempt corporation.
Encounter Books website address: www.encounterbooks.com

Manufactured in the United States and printed on
acid-free paper. The paper used in this publication meets
the minimum requirements of ANSI/NISO Z39.48–1992
(R 1997) (*Permanence of Paper*).

FIRST AMERICAN EDITION

LIBRARY OF CONGRESS CATALOGING-IN-PUBLICATION DATA IS AVAILABLE

Information for this title can be found at the Library of Congress
website under the following ISBN 978-1-64177-361-4 and LCCN 2024002229.

CONTENTS

To all the people who shared their stories with me.
I will never forget your kindness.

PREFACE

I started working on this book when it became clear to me that it was missing. I had written a book called *Bad News: How Woke Media Is Undermining Democracy* about how American journalism had gone from a working-class trade to an elite, over-credentialed caste. Once crusaders on behalf of the have-nots, those locked out of power because they worked with their hands, journalists became the haves, the most overeducated profession in America and part of the economic elite. Over the course of this ascent, they abandoned the concerns and values of the working class to which they once belonged and on whose behalf they once toiled.

Bad News was focused on journalism, but for me, it provided a window into a larger class divide that has come to define the United States, a country we like to think of as a classless society. This class divide has become entrenched: having a college degree is predictive of how long you'll live, how likely you are to own your own home, how healthy you are, and whether your children will be better off than you. As the economists Anne Case and Angus Deaton have pointed out, mortality itself is diverging by education. "Deaths of despair, morbidity, and emotional distress continue to rise in the United States, largely borne by those without a college degree—the majority of American adults—for many of whom the economy and society are no longer delivering," Case and Deaton wrote in 2022 of the two-thirds of Americans without a college education.[1]

The class divide has become the defining characteristic of American life in the twenty-first century. Yet the working class is a cipher in American politics and media. Despite the fact that the largest share of Americans are working class, their voices have essentially been erased from the public sphere and public debate. How do American workers view their chance at the American Dream, their struggles and triumphs, and their place in American society? What do working-class Americans want? What do their lives look like? Do *they* believe they have a fair shot at the American Dream, or do they think that the system is rigged against them? What does the American Dream mean to them?

These are the questions that I have tried to answer in *Second Class: How the Elites Betrayed America's Working Men and Women*. I spent a year traveling around the country interviewing working-class people to get their sense of whether they had a shot at the American Dream, and if not, what might make it more of a reality, or even a possibility. I spoke to people from across the political spectrum, people of different genders and races and family structures and religious creeds from all over the country. It is their stories you will read in what follows.

I went into this project expecting to find a situation that was dire. My own friendship and family circles included a lot of people in the higher strata of the working class, people who were either solidly middle class or close to it. But I assumed my friends and family members were unrepresentative. I expected to find that the deaths of despair described by Case and Deaton were the norm, and I initially gave the book the title *Unpromised Land* because of the broken compact it seemed to me we had made with working people.

What I found was a much more complex picture. People do believe they can achieve the American Dream. But they have to work twice as hard to achieve half as much as their parents did, or as the college-educated caste working in the knowledge industry do. And still, many lives are defined by precariousness.

A few things came up in nearly every one of the interviews I did, which also surprised me. The first of those was the value of hard work. I can't think of a single person I interviewed who didn't tell me that working hard is a value they learned as children and is central to their identity. Work means dignity and independence and autonomy and pride. It means having something no one can take away from you, even when work is scarce, even when the conditions aren't ideal. The Marxist view of work as inherently exploitative, something people would ideally be freed from, has taken on new life on the American Left as well as the free-market Right, with ideas like Universal Basic Income. But the working-class Americans I spoke to over the past year didn't view work as exploitative. They viewed the value of hard work through an almost spiritual lens, as though it were a precious inheritance that continued to connect them with their parents, who as children they saw getting up every morning and going out to provide for their families. It is essential to how they see themselves as Americans, and a great source of pride, no matter what they did for a living.

The flip side of the dignity of work is the impatience that most of the people I spoke to have for people they view as choosing *not* to work and living off government benefits—and the corresponding inability of working families to get the little help they need which would make their lives so much less stressful. No one I spoke to wanted to live off the government, temporarily or permanently. They didn't think big government was the answer, and spoke frequently about government waste and welfare fraud, things they saw a lot of firsthand. What they did want was a system that rewarded those who work hard, who still can't get a foothold in the middle class.

As for who could get them there, I found a deep distrust of both political parties. The Democrats were seen as the party of the educated elites and the dependent poor, the party behind the mechanism that conveyed their hard-earned tax dollars to people defrauding the system. But the Republicans were seen as the party of the rich, the party of corporations, the side pimping out the working class to achieve the goals of conservative elites.

The majority of the people I spoke to have views that don't fit with either party. Whether liberal or conservative, most people I spoke to supported significantly limiting immigration but also majorly expanding access to health care. They supported gay marriage and were very pro-gay, but also very worried about the spread of transgender ideology, especially the spread in schools. They were "anti-woke," but it wasn't a topic they thought about a lot; instead, they thought a lot about housing, and why they couldn't afford it. An extreme moderation, tolerance, and practicality threaded itself through their views. For example, I heard often from women that they personally opposed abortion but they could understand why someone would get one, and they were very much against the idea of banning it.

Most of all, the people I spoke to across the board were appalled at the divisiveness of our politics, when they themselves were part of such a politically, ideologically, racially, and religiously diverse world. Working-class Americans simply don't have the luxury of hating people for their political beliefs—nor do they have the appetite for it.

Every person I interviewed for this book had a unique story and perspective. The stories I ended up including in what follows reflect people whose circumstances seemed to me to represent a larger piece of the puzzle in the portrait I was trying to paint of the working class. The words in italics in part 1 are derived from direct quotes from my interview subjects, things they told me they thought about frequently. In part 2, I used quotation marks to reflect their direct quotes, because their quotes in part 2 are interspersed with quotes from experts and my own analysis.

I am deeply grateful to everyone who shared his or her story with me for this book. Some names and identifying features have been changed to maintain anonymity for people who feared they would lose their jobs. I also committed a journalistic crime and paid some of the respondents for their time, which is common for academics but a big no-no for journalists. I just couldn't bring myself to ask people whose only asset is their time to give it to me for free. In fact, lots of the subjects in this book became friends, another big journalistic taboo. I was constantly aware of my own immense privilege while speaking to people whose lives are so much harder than mine, and in more ways than one, I couldn't help but try to do more than most journalists consider prudent. I admit to you my sins so you can judge them for yourself before proceeding.

PART 1

Who Is the American Working Class?

INTRODUCTION
TO PART 1

The roads are black and empty at 4:15 in the morning when Gord Magill sets out for what will be a thirteen-hour workday in his truck. It's early summer in Upstate New York, and up in the sky, Venus, Jupiter, Mars, and Saturn have taken to lining up in a neat little formation running from one side of Gord's massive windshield to the other. It's the kind of sight that makes a man feel his insignificance acutely. *When you get up real early, you have some intimate contact with the heavens*, Gord thinks, one of the fringe benefits of his job. He thinks about other unfathomable night skies he's seen throughout his career as a trucker—the aurora borealis in Alberta, the massive night sky of the Australian Outback. By the time the sun rises, Gord's windshield will be covered in the tiny bodies of recently hatched flies, as numerous as the stars. For now, it's still sparkling clean from having been washed the night before. The planets blink at him in the moonlight.

To hit the road by 4:15, Gord woke up at 3:15, showered, and packed a lunch—butternut squash and lentil soup in a thermos, kippers, an energy bar, a flask of cold-brew coffee heated on the stove, and three bottles of water. Then he quietly closed the door behind him so as not to wake his wife Jenna, a schoolteacher, and their two little girls.

By 4:15, he is driving his cab to pick up the rig from the wood mill, from where he'll start the two-hour drive to the Catskills to pick up a haul of lumber, what they call a "cleanup load." His rig can carry up to twenty-four tons of wood. He'll drive two hours back to the mill to drop off his load before going back for a second one. Then the day's work will be done and he can shower for the second time and have dinner with Jenna and the girls.

Gord is one of 3.5 million truckers in America. In a post-pandemic economy, trucking is at an all-time high, one of the top ten most common jobs in America. Trucking is in Gord's bones: his dad is a trucker, and his granddad was one too, driving a truck through Europe during the war for the Canadian army, something Gord is proud of. Trucking suits him with its long, quiet hours. He has taken a few breaks over the years to do construction, being good with his hands. He recently built a wooden picnic bench for the backyard of the house they rent from Jenna's brother. But somehow, Gord always found himself back in the truck. There was a lot of dealing with other people in construction—the contractor and the other employees. Gord missed being left alone.

He used to work for a big corporation, but they didn't treat him well. They refused to tell him where he was headed the night before, and when he made suggestions about how they could improve things for drivers, he was accused of being sexist, because the head of HR was a woman. And there was also a lot of surveillance, which was totally anathema to what he loved about the job. He vowed never to work for a big corporation again, with their human resources and safety departments that seemed to see workers like him as little more than a potential insurance claim.

So Gord took a $10,000 pay cut and went to work for a small operation, a go-between who buys from loggers and sells to mills. After a logger cuts down a bunch of trees, they call Gord's boss, and he comes and scales the haul, measuring the logs for diameter and length and imperfections. Then he grades the haul and sends Gord to pick it up. Gord hauls oak, maple, ash, soft maple, cherry, and occasionally hickory back to the mills, and they sell it to people who make it into kitchen cabinets or flooring.

Back on the road, Gord thinks about the strange dream he had last night: He'd been loading and unloading a barge and trying to make sure the girls were on it, or off it, he couldn't quite remember. But it isn't his dreams that keep him up at night. It's the knowledge that no matter how many long hours he works hauling lumber, no matter how much backbreaking driving and loading he puts in, he will never be able to afford to buy his own home, something he can leave to his girls.

Between Gord's wages and Jenna's, they are just clearing their monthly bills. Gord and Jenna both make about $50,000 a year. For Gord, who works thirteen-hour shifts five days a week, that's just about $15 an hour. Jenna's parents help a lot with the girls, and their rent is reasonable, thanks to Jenna's brother owning their home. But it's still not enough to save anything. And the home prices where they live are astronomical.

We don't have it bad, Gord quickly corrects himself. He doesn't want to be one of those people complaining about how unlucky they are. A lot of people are deep in debt and have to doggy paddle just to keep up. He and Jenna have enough to cover their bills. Their girls are fed. They own a car and a pickup truck. But by the time rent, taxes, childcare, fuel, and energy have been taken out of their paychecks, how is he supposed to save enough for a down payment? And that bothers him because he knows that the key to passing on a better life to the next generation is to be able to give your children land and a house, leverage to pay for school or whatever they want to pursue in the future. *We don't have that.*

A lot of people don't. Driving in the early hours of the dawn that morning, Gord thinks about the fellowship he belongs to, the millions of Americans on whose backs our modern economy is built who don't get paid overtime, who work ten, twelve, fourteen, fifteen hours a day, sixty-plus hours a week all year round in all kinds of weather at backbreaking work. Though the entire economy relies on their labor, and they work and work and work, they have been cut out of the American Dream.

Nicole Day is forty-two years old, but she doesn't have any teeth. Since getting COVID, she's had congestive heart failure, which resulted in an infection that caused all her teeth to be pulled out. But implants cost $50,000, and there's only one dentist in the county who takes the insurance she has—Medicaid, which she has for the next two years only because of her son. She's been waiting six months and still doesn't have an appointment or any sense of when she'll be able to smile again without blushing.

To make ends meet, Nicole drives for DoorDash. She also cleans houses and babysits whenever she can. But even so, she has to make decisions every month about which bills to pay and which to push off, facing late fees or payment plans. Her rent is $1,000 a month, but in a good month, she and her husband, who also drives for DoorDash, only bring in about $1,300, leaving just $300 for groceries, gas, payments for her phone and her son's, and whatever he needs for school. Nicole also takes care of her elderly parents, so she can't move anywhere with better job opportunities. And because of her illness, she can't get a good-paying job. The ones she's qualified for, ones that don't require a college degree, won't let her take off once every few months for her doctor's visits.

Nicole has noticed that if you don't have a college degree, you don't have opportunities. *It's hard for people that are intelligent that don't have a degree. We can bring something to the table. We just don't get the same opportunities as other people.* That's what Nicole wants: opportunity for lower-income people. She doesn't want more government benefits. She doesn't want charity. She believes in hard work, and she works very hard. She dreams of a job where she feels she's contributing something, like she's helping elevate the people around her. But she's found it impossible to find.

Nicole is part of the 10 percent of Americans who make between $15,000 and $24,000 a year, despite working as hard as she can, as many hours as she can. She has nothing left over to save or for emergency expenses. She doesn't qualify for Section 8 because she and her husband make too much. They only have one car, though, so they have to take turns working. Her husband's car broke down, then her car broke down, and because she has no money to fix it, she's driving her dad's car, which has no windows; she's driving for DoorDash in a car whose windows are covered in cardboard.

If she could just find a job that pays $16 an hour and nets her $35,000 or $40,000 a year, she'd have more than enough. All of her financial stress would disappear. But those kinds of jobs don't have a clause for people who contracted heart failure during COVID and need to spend one workday every three months at the doctor. At least, that's been Nicole's experience.

So instead, she drives for DoorDash, which means her wages vary dramatically from day to day, making it harder to plan. Some days she makes $20, some days she makes $100. She works for DoorDash six-to-ten hours a day, depending on which bills are coming up. DoorDash pays $2.25 per order, and then there are tips. So if somebody tips you $3 and they live fifteen minutes away, you're making $5.25. Every now and again you'll get the $10 or $11 order and that will make up for the $5 order. Before gas, Nicole averages about $18 an hour, but by the time she's paid for gas, it comes down to about $13.

It's just not enough to feel any kind of stability, no matter how many hours she puts in. She's already on an installment plan with the electric company because back in December she couldn't pay her bill. The company broke down the $500 she owed into

$97 installments, which it now adds onto her monthly bill each subsequent month.

Her life is constant work and constant stress. But somehow, the bills always get paid. The hardest part, the part that brings tears to her eyes, is thinking about her son, how he asks her for things, and she just can't do it. *He's such a great kid. He understands.* He always tells her, "I understand, Mom. It's fine."

If Nicole had a megaphone to the most powerful people in this country, here's what she'd say: *Just give us a chance. Give us more opportunity. We need some help and not just handout stuff. We need a boost. It's not about giving me stuff for free. I don't want that. I want better opportunities and more opportunities.*

But it's more natural for her to think about what she'd tell someone in her situation, what she tells herself every day: *Don't give up and keep pushing. There's always, always a rainbow. Don't give up. You gotta fight for your kids.*

———

Doug Tansy is living the American Dream. A forty-five-year-old Native Alaskan, Doug is an electrician living in Fairbanks in a house he and his wife Kristine own. Kristine has a social work degree, but for thirteen years, she was able to stay home to raise their five children, thanks to Doug's wages and benefits, secured by the International Brotherhood of Electrical Workers. All of Doug's union friends have similar stories; those who chose not to have kids traveled the world on the money they earned.

Doug started an apprenticeship right out of high school, one of the best things he ever did for himself. It was something he did for *himself*: his high school pushed everyone to go to college, which Doug did, too, but to pay for his first year, he took a summer job working construction. He got the job thanks to his Native connections; the Alaska Native Claims Settlement Act of 1970 transferred titles to more than 200 regional and local village corporations, and Doug is a shareholder for two of those corporations on his mom's side and one on his dad's side. Members of those corporations helped him find that first summer construction job. He got important skills on the job, but even more important was the contrast it provided with his college courses the following year. College was challenging, but it didn't excite him. It didn't challenge him in the way he wanted to be challenged, in a way that made him want to show up and do it again and again. Construction did. It grabbed him. Doug was always told to find what your hands want to do and when you do, to do that with all your might. So he did.

Doug's father was a heavy equipment operator. His mom was a teacher. When he decided he wanted to leave college to do electrical work, he had plenty of guidance. The apprenticeship was 8,000 hours of on-the-job training and 1,490 hours of classroom training. He started his career debt free and with four different retirement funds. Doug chuckles when he remembers that he had to take out a $10,000 loan from his bank just to start building credit because he had no debt. He paid it right back.

Doug now serves as the assistant business manager of the IBEW in Fairbanks and as president of the Fairbanks Central Labor Council, which is sort of like the local chapter of the AFL-CIO. The union is diverse—ethnically but also ideologically: there are Republicans, independents, Democrats, progressives, and everything in between. And certainly, there is disagreement. Debates can get testy, especially when social issues like abortion come up in the break room. Doug has experienced racism on rare occasions, too. And yet, there is a deep bond connecting the members of the IBEW that transcends ideological lines; Doug calls the union a fraternity and sorority. If he ever got in trouble, he knows he can make one phone call and that's the only call he'll need to make. His brothers and sisters will take care of the rest, and whatever he needs will be coming.

That bond is the result of a simple fact: more unites them than divides them, and what unites them is sacred. *Having good wages and benefits and good conditions, being treated fairly and with dignity in retirement, should not be only for Republicans or Democrats or red states or blue states. These are nonpartisan issues that should be for everybody.*

Doug is a registered Democrat, but he actively works to combat the politicization of his union. He surrounds himself with conservatives and independents, people who will check him. He insists that there be a conservative voice at the table, at every table, debating with him and decision-making with him because left to his own devices, he knows he will go too far.

Yet the experience Doug works to secure for his fellow electricians is getting rarer and rarer. Despite the benefits they provide, fewer Americans than ever belong to unions, a scant 6 percent of Americans working in the private sector. Many believe that they are a dying institution.

Even worse is the fact that the trades in general have gotten a bad rap. People perceive the trades as a fallback if you're not capable of doing college. *It's hurting us as a society*, Doug thinks, *how little effort is going into steering kids in the direction of the trades.* The security he has is something he wishes everyone could have, something everyone *should* have access to, yet somehow, so few do. There are a lot of people in this country that have a raw deal of it, that are losing ground in terms of wages and benefits.

It's not just about those struggling families. It's about his own. If the other families in his community are struggling, if those homes aren't safe, if there is substance abuse and downward mobility, where are Doug's children going to play? *We have so much more in common than we disagree about*, Doug thinks often. *And through that, we can elevate ourselves, our community, our state, our nation, and we all win.*

Gord, Nicole, and Doug are all members of America's working class, a sector of society as diverse as it is large. They all work at jobs that don't require a college degree, use their labor to earn their living, and they aren't part of the top 20 percent. But they are also representative of larger divisions within the working class. Many working-class Americans working in the trades are like Doug—living solidly middle-class lives if you think of middle class as a lifestyle: they are homeowners whose children are upwardly mobile, and they will be able to retire in dignity. Many others, like Gord, are able to cover their bills but have no savings. For them, homeownership is a distant fantasy. And many working-class Americans spend their lives teetering on the edge of grinding poverty, like Nicole.

The radical diversity of the American working class makes it challenging to answer some basic questions: Who is the American working class? Do they still have a fair shot at the American Dream? Nestled between the dependent poor and the upper-class elites, working-class Americans make up the bulk of our society, and yet their struggles and aspirations remain opaque to those who set the agenda for the nation.

Maybe this is why Americans without a college degree, the backbone of this country, have been left out of the kind of prosperity that college-educated Americans have started to take for granted. While working longer hours and producing more in terms of GDP than ever before, working-class wages have stagnated, and even modest recent gains are no longer able to provide the hallmarks of a middle-class life and the American Dream: homeownership, a retirement in dignity, an education for one's children.

Once upon a time in the not-so-distant past, you didn't need a college degree to ensure these things. But the middle class has

Figure 1: Productivity, Profit, and GDP Have Risen in Lockstep Since the 1960s, While Wages Have Stagnated

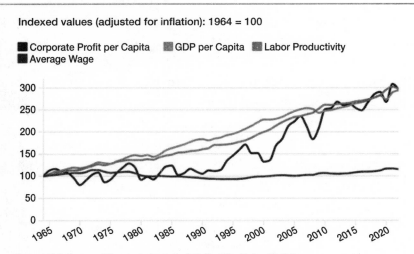

Indexed values (adjusted for inflation): 1964 = 100

■ Corporate Profit per Capita   ■ GDP per Capita   ■ Labor Productivity
■ Average Wage

Source: U.S. Bureau of Economic Analysis, U.S. Bureau of Labor Statistics
Profit = Corporate Profits After Tax with Inventory Valuation Adjustment and Capital Consumption Adjustment (adjusted for inflation with the Consumer Price Index); GDP = Real Gross Domestic Product (chained 2012 dollars); Productivity = Nonfarm Business Labor Productivity (output per hour); Wage = Real Average Earnings of Production and Nonsupervisory Workers (adjusted for inflation with the Consumer Price Index.

Figure 1. Productivity, profit, and GDP compared to wages, 1965–2020. American Compass, "Rebuilding American Capitalism."

been steadily losing ground since the 1970s. Free-market types like to point out that at the same time, GDP has risen, and that's true. It has, as have profits and productivity. The only thing that has stagnated are the wages of the workers creating that profit for their bosses. While corporate profit, productivity, and GDP have risen by 200 percent since 1965, wages have risen by a measly 1 percent, as you can see in figure 1, an analysis of data from the U.S. Bureau of Economic Analysis and the U.S. Bureau of Labor Statistics put together by American Compass, a think tank devoted to creating a U.S. economy that uplifts families and communities.

Why did working-class wages stagnate? A number of factors played a role. Before 1970, the biggest sector of the U.S. economy was manufacturing; a quarter of our nation's wealth was once generated there, where workers got great health care, excellent wages, and a pension.[1] Fast forward to 2022 and the biggest share of the U.S. economy—one-fifth of it—is in finance, real estate, and insurance, parts of the economy that make money off Wall Street speculation rather than production and which cut the American worker out of the picture. Manufacturing, meanwhile, makes up just 11 percent of today's economy.

While the majority of Americans are working class, their wages represent an increasingly smaller piece of the economic pie, reducing their power in the marketplace by leaps and bounds. Until the 1970s, American workers labored in factories making things—cars, homes—that they and their neighbors consumed, which created a natural upper limit on prices and profit because they weren't just producers but consumers. The profits from their labor were reinvested into the factories and into them, the workers, to make sure they could keep buying the products they made; after all, they were the biggest share of the market. But in an economy where the biggest share of the money is being made in speculation by a tiny percent of people who own or control most of the investments, the worker gets a vanishingly small slice of the pie.

Meanwhile, as good manufacturing jobs started to be shipped *en masse* overseas, the U.S. saw a flood of immigrants willing to work for lower pay than American workers here at home. Back in 1970, the high-water mark for working-class wages, immigrants represented less than 5 percent of the total U.S. population. Today, immigrants account for 13 percent of the U.S. population, closing in on the highest it's ever been, which was in 1890—not coincidentally, another era characterized by extreme inequality.[2] Without manufacturing, American workers were left to do jobs you couldn't offshore in the service industry, which pay much less than a factory where the worker's ability to buy what he or she makes is what keeps the lights on—and then those service industry jobs were undercut by a glut of illegal labor.

In 1994, these trends were radically accelerated when then president Bill Clinton signed the North American Free Trade Agreement, perhaps the single most impactful piece of legislation on workers over the past fifty years. As a result of this new trade deal, industrial working-class jobs that secured factory workers with wages on a par with college professors were largely shipped away to China and Mexico, while the U.S. began pursuing trade that favored workers in other countries. It resulted in decimated communities across the Rust Belt and the Midwest.

The Right likes to point out that thanks to globalization, flat-screen TVs, iPhones, and even food items are cheaper, increasing the purchasing power of working-class Americans. Yet their purchasing power when it comes to securing the hallmarks of a middle-class life have plummeted, because the cost of the items that secure that life—a home, health care, a dignified retirement—have grown astronomically.

The cost of a home has doubled in the U.S. since 1970, though in some states—notably California and Washington—it's risen by much more, 250 percent and 352 percent, respectively.[3] The cost of health care has risen from 5 percent of GDP in 1960 to 20 percent in 2021, from $146 a year per capita to a staggering $12,000, though we are less healthy than ever. And the average cost of college has jumped by 3,000 percent, making the average college tuition thirty-one times what it was in 1969.[4]

These aren't random ways of measuring a middle-class life. When American Compass surveyed American families in 2023, they found that there was broad consensus about the essential components of a middle-class life: comprehensive health insurance, owning a home, being able to support a child on one income, and being able to send your kid to college, as you can see in figure 2.[5] Meanwhile, a large majority felt rising inequality, stagnating wages, and losing the option for one parent to stay home and raise the kids was a big problem.

Figure 2: Defining Middle Class in America

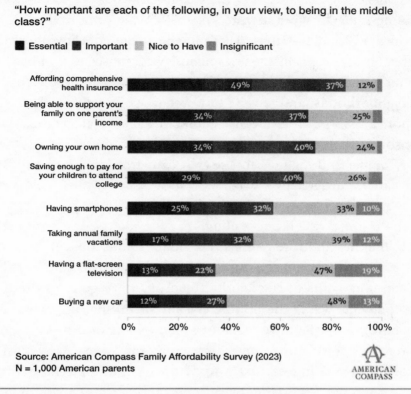

"How important are each of the following, in your view, to being in the middle class?"

■ Essential ■ Important ▨ Nice to Have ■ Insignificant

Affording comprehensive health insurance	49%	37%	12%
Being able to support your family on one parent's income	34%	37%	25%
Owning your own home	34%	40%	24%
Saving enough to pay for your children to attend college	29%	40%	26%
Having smartphones	25%	32%	33% 10%
Taking annual family vacations	17%	32%	39% 12%
Having a flat-screen television	13% 22%	47%	19%
Buying a new car	12% 27%	48%	13%

0%   20%   40%   60%   80%   100%

Source: American Compass Family Affordability Survey (2023)
N = 1,000 American parents

AMERICAN COMPASS

Figure 2. How Americans define being middle class. Courtesy of American Compass, "Rebuilding American Capitalism."

Perhaps most damning was the finding that Americans making $40,000–$60,000 a year were as worried about affording health care, a home, a car, and tuition as parents making less than $20,000. This precariousness—the lack of stability and constant feeling of teetering on the edge—persists even when wages rise, because the cost of the markers of middle-class stability has risen exponentially more.

At least some of the exploding costs of a middle-class life are the result of the two-family income coupled with the fact that college-educated men and women now tend to marry each other, when in previous generations they would marry people without a college degree, spreading the wealth. This has created not just rising inequality but a caste system in which married college-educated couples with two combined college-educated incomes are competing against single-income working-class families for a smaller and smaller stock of housing in ever-more expensive neighborhoods, and fewer and fewer spots in colleges that cost more and more. They are also competing against each other with incomes that keep rising, driving up the costs of a middle-class life higher and higher because they can afford them. Before she became a progressive, Elizabeth Warren called this the "two-income trap."

Progressives like to rail against the 1 percent, those people making about ten times the median household income of $67,000 a year. But the truth is that a huge proportion of the economic gains of the last half century have gone to the top 20 percent. While the middle class is shrinking, not everyone is falling into the lower classes; at least some of those who are no longer middle income are now upper income. Many with a college degree in jobs that would have been middle class thirty years ago are now in the top fifth percentile. In the 1970s, it was middle-class families who earned the largest chunk of America's income. Today, it's the upper middle class, or the educated elites, as you can see in figure 3.

A college education is tightly correlated with getting into that upper-class tier. College-educated Americans make on average $1.2 million more than working-class Americans throughout the course of their career, while Americans with a doctoral or professional degree average $3 million more, as Stephen J. Rose found in his 2020 report *Social Stratification in the United States*.[6] Just 5 percent of Americans with a graduate degree make less than $37,000 a year—compared to 37 percent of Americans with a high school diploma. Thirty-six

Figure 3: Share of Aggregate Income Held by U.S. Middle Class has Plunged Since 1970

Share of aggregate income held by U.S. middle class has plunged since 1970

% of U.S. aggregate household income held by lower-, middle- and upper-income households

Figure 3. The plunging share of GDP held by the middle class. "The American Middle Class Is Losing Ground," Pew Research Center, December 9, 2015.

percent of college grads make between $185,000 and $222,000 a year—compared to just 13 percent of high-school educated Americans.[7]

And much of the research shows that the dividing line between Americans who are able to snatch the rewards of today's economy and those who aren't is a college degree. Instead of a pathway for upward mobility, college has become the gatekeeper of it. Indeed, because so much of this success is allocated to Americans based on whether or not they have a college degree, many define class using this metric. Class, of course, is not just about money. It's about culture, geography, even communal values. But many of those things now work together in tandem as predictors of economic stability and an escape from the precariousness of working-class life.

As Richard V. Reeves put it in *Dream Hoarders: How the American Upper Middle Class Is Leaving Everyone Else in the Dust, Why That Is a Problem, and What to Do about It,*

> Class is not just about money, though it is about that. The class gap can be seen from every angle: education, security, family, health, you name it. There will also be inequalities on each of these dimensions, of course. But inequality becomes class division when all these varied elements—money, education, wealth, occupation—cluster together so tightly that, in practice, almost any one of them will suffice for the purposes of class definition. Class division becomes class stratification when these advantages—and thus status—endure across generations. In fact, upper-middle-class status is passed down to the next generation more effectively than in the past, and in the United States more than in other countries.

The new heritability of class has led others researching the working class to define class based on whether someone's parents have a degree, or whether their father had a college degree, as Jennifer M. Silva does in *Coming Up Short: Working-Class Adulthood in an Age of Uncertainty.*

Still others have used an economic metric for defining working class. In 2018, an American Enterprise Institute report compiled by Robert Doar, Ryan Streeter, and W. Bradford Wilcox defined the working class as people with at least a high-school diploma but less than a four-year college degree who had a household income of $30,000 to $69,000 a year for two adults and one child.[8] Others define working class based on occupation—on whether an occupation requires a college degree or not, whether the occupation is part of the service economy as opposed to the knowledge economy, or whether it involves labor versus management. For Nicholas Wolfinger, a professor of sociology at the University of

Utah who studies the family, the working class is everyone who isn't a four-year college graduate who's been locked out of the top 20 percent of the income distribution—which in today's dollars would be a salary of about $130,000 a year.

That's the definition I found most compelling in writing this book, which is why you will find an overlap between working class and middle class described here. The people you will meet described in this book are working class in that they belong to the sector of American society that works in jobs that require physical labor or social, caretaking skills rather than whatever it is people claim you learn in college (though some of them have a college degree), who haven't managed to become rich. But some of them, as you will see in the chapters that follow, have made it into the middle class, which I use in this book as a description of a lifestyle that includes a home, a retirement, adequate health care, and greater opportunities for one's children—in other words, the American Dream.

The reason I settled on this definition is because of the overwhelming evidence that a college degree represents *the* dividing line separating the working class from the elites, so a book about what ails us would be wise to focus on that all-too-invisible fault line. But just how deep is that divide?

Consider the work of economists Anne Case and Angus Deaton. Case and Deaton coined the phrase "deaths of despair" to reflect the exploding number of deaths by alcoholism, drug overdose, and suicide that's plaguing working-class Americans. "Deaths of despair, morbidity, and emotional distress continue to rise in the United States, largely borne by those without a college degree—the majority of American adults—for many of whom the economy and society are no longer delivering," Case and Deaton wrote in 2022.[9] Life expectancy has been dropping in the U.S. for the first time in fifty years, but the entirety of that decline has been in the working class.[10] And working-class people aren't just dying more; they are more likely to have chronic pain, less likely to go to church or be married, and they drink much more.

"While the college wage premium has soared to unprecedented levels, the inequality between these two groups involves much more than money," write Case and Deaton.[11] "The college degree has now become 'a condition of dignified work and of social esteem'...as well as a matter of life and death, with adult life expectancy rising for the college educated and falling for the rest."

This is not to say that having a college degree ensures you the American Dream. There are plenty of millennials in good paying jobs living in D.C. where homeownership is out of reach. Meanwhile, 11 percent of service-industry jobs are done by people with a college degree. College-educated Starbucks baristas working in Brooklyn, New York, are not homeowners. But a lot of the people working service-industry jobs who have a degree are not looking at a lifetime of such work.

We're often told that millennials are the first generation to make less than their parents. Yet here again, the class divide is crucial: millennials with a bachelor's degree or higher actually make *more* than other generations did between the ages of twenty-five and thirty-seven. It's those with just some college or a high-school degree that make significantly less. The median household income for a millennial with a college degree between the ages of twenty-five and thirty-seven in 2018 was $105,000 a year, compared to just $62,000 for someone that age with some college but no degree and $49,000 for a millennial with no college at all.

Moreover, college-educated millennials are significantly more likely to be homeowners than those without a college degree.[12] And while it takes millennials longer to acquire homes than older generations, that gap closes as they age; at age forty, for example, the homeownership of millennials is 60 percent, just three points behind Gen X.

No doubt, there are Americans with a college degree who are struggling—like Oshrat, a Maryland teacher who's a single mom and just barely scraping by. Oshrat makes $44,000 a year with which she supports herself and her three children. And though she was lucky enough to get a mortgage through a program that no longer exists, she has no retirement savings and no hope of getting any. Every month is a struggle to pay the bills, and she frequently ends up having to ask for help, from friends or her rabbi, or family members. She considers it a miracle every month when there is enough food for the family and the electricity bill is paid off.

But many more college grads are doing well, either on their way or already in the top fifth percentile and upwardly mobile. It is their counterparts without a college degree in the service industry whose lives are much more precarious than those of previous generations.

And yet, though the diploma divide is crucial to understanding America today, it can also obscure some important truths about the working class. The truth is, many Americans without a college degree *are* in fact living solidly middle-class lives, while many have lives as precarious as those of Americans living at or below the poverty line.

Consider Patrick, an NYPD detective who owns his own home and whose daughter is currently in college. Patrick is a cop, but he's also an artist who spends his free time in his basement painting huge, detailed murals depicting the heartbreak of being Black and a police officer. Detective Patrick believes he's found the formula for the American Dream: hard work. If you ask him what he needs from America, he will tell you he needs nothing.

Now think about Amy, a certified nurse's aide. Amy lives in Florida with her longtime partner, also a nurse's aide. While they are able to pay their bills, the idea of homeownership is simply not on the table. The price of a home where they live is astronomical.

Amy makes $22 an hour, and she doesn't think she will ever own her own home. Saving is impossible these days, especially with inflation, and her deductible is so high that she spends all her savings on health care every year. Amy lives in a home owned by her partner's mother. If you ask Amy what she and her fellow CNAs need, she would tell you two things: housing and unions.

Now consider Maria. Maria works as a home health aide caring for her mother-in-law in Reno. But though her mother-in-law has dementia and requires round-the-clock care, she only gets twenty-five hours of paid care a week, and that pays a paltry $11 an hour, which means that though Maria spends every waking hour on call or actively caring for her mother-in-law, she is forced to subsist on wages that don't begin to cover her bills. And even though her husband works for General Motors, they are constantly behind, making calls to the electric company to beg forbearance.

From a certain point of view, Patrick, Amy, and Maria are all working class. They all work in professions that don't require a college degree, though Patrick has one. Yet their lives are also extremely different in ways that represent larger segments of the working class. There are three main groups: I call them struggling, floating, and rising.

Americans like Patrick and Doug—police officers, sanitation workers, electricians, plumbers, people who work in the energy sector, and many skilled tradesfolk—fall into the category of the rising working class. By and large, these are working-class Americans who have accessed the American Dream and are living solidly middle-class lives: They own their own homes, they look forward to retiring with dignity, and their children are likely to be as financially secure as they are.

There are also many working-class Americans like Amy and Gord—CNAs and truckers and stockers and Amazon workers and nurses' assistants—who have enough to cover their expenses but will never be able to buy a home, that access point to the kind of financial security that will ensure their children are upwardly mobile. Many live in metro areas where the price of a home has skyrocketed. They worry they won't be able to retire. This is the floating working class.

And then there are the working poor, struggling working-class Americans—cashiers and retail salespersons and waiters and home health aids and fast-food workers and DoorDashers—who are the most precarious. The ranks of these workers are filled with single mothers and grandmothers, those least likely to be able to secure upward mobility for their children, people whose lives are at highest risk of violent crime or addiction. They often lie awake at night staring at the ceiling and wondering whether the next bill that comes in will spell disaster for them and their families.

How many Americans are in each of these groups? It's hard to say. But this three-tiered breakdown reflects a larger one in American society. The Financial Health Network found that if you calculated people's financial health based on things such as do they spend less than they earn, pay bills on time, have long-term savings and manageable debt, you find that 15 percent are financially vulnerable, 55 percent are financially coping, and 31 percent are financially healthy.[13]

When it comes to Americans in the service industry or making $20,000 to $80,000 a year, you can see a similar distribution of income, as illustrated in figure 4.

Figure 4. Distribution of Wages in the Service Industry.

$20,000–$30,000	15.34%
$30,000–$40,000	15.18%
$40,000–$50,000	15.52%
$50,000–$60,000	15.06%
$60,000–$70,000	14.74%
$70,000–$80,000	13.82%

From the American Community Survey, 2020, prepared by Dr. Joe Price, Katherine Wilson, and Megan McQueen at Brigham Young University.

Of course, a lot depends on where you live. Earning $65,000 a year will get you a lot farther in West Virginia than it will in San Francisco. As Edward Pinto at the American Enterprise Institute has pointed out, in 2020, the price-to-income ratio of a home in California was double what it was in the rest of the country; it took the median worker eight times their income to purchase a home. Yet there are counties across the nation—mostly in the middle, in rural and red America—where the ratio is more like three.

If you define the American Dream by the rate of homeownership for the working class, the American Dream is alive and well in many red states, while it's limping along in blue states, by and large due to the cost of housing. And it's not just in rural areas. Of the ten metro areas with the worst homeownership rates for young people between the ages of twenty-five to thirty-five, seven are in California and two more are in New York. West Virginia has the highest homeownership rate in the nation, with Alabama, Indiana, and Pennsylvania also in the top twenty states.

The geographical housing divide helps explain how 51 percent of the 1.7 million Americans employed as maids or housekeeping cleaners who make up 5 percent of the service industry own their own homes, as you can see in figure 5.

Figure 5. The Homeownership Rate of Certain Working-Class Occupations.

OCCUPATION WITHIN SERVICE INDUSTRY	TOTAL IN INDUSTRY	HOMEOWNERSHIP (BY OCCUPATION)
Maids and Housekeeping Cleaners	1,727,413	51.39%
Waiters and Waitresses	2,041,931	52.10%
Food Servers, Nonrestaurant	220,750	57.09%
Food preparation and serving related workers, nec	285,609	58.78%
Dishwashers	320,865	45.83%
Police Officers and Detectives	1,112,437	83.11%
Firefighters	388,672	81.15%
Sheriffs, Bailiffs, Correctional Officers, and Jailers	456,121	76.24%

From the American Community Survey, 2020, prepared by Dr. Joe Price, Katherine Wilson, and Megan McQueen at Brigham Young University.

Of the two million waiters and waitresses working in America, just over half own their homes.[14] Just under half of all dishwashers own the home they live in.[15] Of course, that number is much higher for firefighters (81 percent own their homes), police officers (83 percent own their homes), and correctional officers (76 percent own their homes). But even the numbers for lower-paying working-class jobs are much higher than you might expect, largely due to the varying cost of housing across the nation.

If you look at a heat map of Americans earning $20,000 to $80,000 a year and compare 2000 to 2021, you can see the middle class disappearing. California, Seattle, Maine, and Florida all used to have solid, stable middle-class populations of over 57 percent of the state. Today, they are barely cracking 50 percent.

It's the disappearing middle class in two maps, as shown in figure 6 on the next page.

Though a middle-class life is still attainable for a wide range of Americans, the number is falling. According to data from the American Community Survey, compiled by Dr. Joe Price, Katherine Wilson, and Megan McQueen at Brigham Young University, the homeownership rate of service industry workers fell from 58 percent to 54 percent between 2000 and 2020.[16] For Americans working in warehousing and transportation, it fell from 65 percent to 59 percent. Meanwhile, the homeownership rate of Black Americans in the service industry has plummeted in recent years, from 49 percent to an abysmal 32 percent.

It's not because workers are younger. The working class has also gotten older in that period, with the mean age rising from thirty-nine to fifty-one. In other words, things are getting worse overall; it's not just young people who aren't *yet* homeowners, but older people who aren't on their way into another industry. Yet though the homeownership rate of working-class Americans is shrinking, their number is growing.

Figure 6. The Middle-Class Population by State in 2000 and 2021.

Middle Class Population by State 2000

Percentage of population who earn $20,000 – $80,000 per year (classified as middle class)

< 46%   46% - 48%   48% - 51%   51% - 53%   53% - 55%   55% - 57%   > 57%

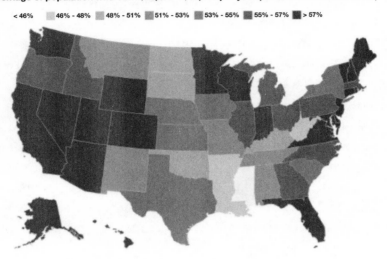

Middle Class Population by State 2021

Percentage of population who earn $20,000 – $80,000 per year (classified as middle class)

< 46%   46% - 48%   48% - 51%   51% - 53%   53% - 55%   55% - 57%   > 57%

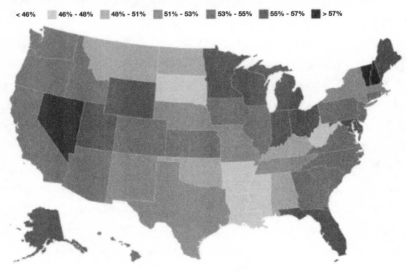

From the American Community Survey, 2020, prepared by Dr. Joe Price, Katherine Wilson, and Megan McQueen at Brigham Young University

In 2000, there were slightly more than twenty-three million Americans employed in service industry jobs. By 2020, that number had increased to thirty million.

Not all of them have been locked out of the middle class. Working-class Americans across a large spectrum of industries *can* access the American Dream—but it means working twice as hard as their parents did and as college-educated Americans do to achieve half as much. And still, it's something of a crapshoot; some will never achieve it, no matter how hard they work, despite doing everything right.

This is how working-class Americans describe their chances at achieving the American Dream: hard work and personal choices can go a long way toward overcoming circumstances and larger, system-wide barriers to success. But you can make all the right choices and work and work and work and still only have a fifty-fifty chance of making it into the middle class.

That's the tragedy of the working-class struggle to achieve the American Dream in the twenty-first century: Working-class Americans have been reduced to second-class citizens, betrayed by the elites who created an economy that rewards the rich and penalizes the poor, who shrank the path to upward mobility to a narrow, precarious bridge.

It's undeniable that in the post-pandemic world, working-class wages are up, in some cases significantly. But for millions and millions of the hardest working Americans, even these better wages are vastly unequal to the cost of purchasing a middle-class life—a home, a vacation here and there, the ability to retire in dignity, adequate health care, and a better future for their kids.

Do working class Americans still have a shot at a middle-class life? They do. But it's a much worse shot than it used to be. That should be unacceptable to us all, no matter our political orientation.

CHAPTER 1

STRUGGLING

O ne of the things that's hardest to comprehend about the richest country on earth is that there are a lot of poor people in it—and a not insignificant portion of them work very hard. A sizeable number of Americans who work full time are so financially unstable that their lives are characterized by insecurity, a constant teetering on the edge of crippling poverty.

In this group are the 4 percent of workers in the U.S. who still make $10 an hour or less. Depending on where they live, they might be part of the 15 percent of Americans making between $20,000 and $30,000 a year. But even many people making $40,000 a year or even $50,000 a year find these wages unequal to the task of raising a family. There are vanishingly few places in the U.S. where this is anything close to a living wage, though they do still exist. Indeed, the federal poverty level is $23,000 a year for a family of three, meaning that many of these workers are working full time yet are still poor, at least by definition.

Worse still, millions of workers rely on some kind of government assistance. Seventy percent of workers receiving government benefits work full-time—most of them in restaurants, department stores, and grocery stores. Of the twelve million working adults enrolled in Medicaid and the nine million working Americans getting food stamps, 70 percent were working thirty-five hours a week or more. "When compared to adult wage earners not participating in the programs, wage-earning adult Medicaid enrollees and SNAP recipients in the private sector were more likely to work in the leisure and hospitality industry and in food service and food preparation occupations," the U.S. Government Accountability Office concluded.[1]

Many view this as a kind of corporate welfare—the U.S. taxpayer footing the bill for corporations that pay starvation wages. But there's also something low-income Americans know as the benefits cliff: people being forced to decline better pay or more hours because they would lose essential government benefits that they can't afford to live without. It puts people into an impossible position of choosing between, for example, excellent government health care that their child depends on and a better paying job with a much worse health care plan. Factor in the skyrocketing costs of health insurance and you see what a bind working people are in.

These people are sinking. And their struggle is often invisible. Facing severe economic hardship can be deeply isolating. For many, it's embarrassing, and the shame creates a taboo around talking about it. This silence is also convenient for the better-off, who would rather not contemplate the difficulty of the lives of those who provide services for them. It makes it almost impossible for us to really grasp what it means to work and work and work and still be destitute, on the verge of homelessness—or even actually homeless.

Having a college degree does not always protect you from this fate. Colissa is a forty-nine-year-old teacher in Athens, Georgia. She was raised in a two-parent household in a home her parents owned, but somehow, the middle-class stability she grew up with has eluded her. Though she has never struggled to find work, she has often found herself at the mercy of the shelter system, so much so that it's become a kind of normal. Resilient and independent, Colissa has learned to roll with the punches, dusting herself off when she's knocked down, and plotting her next move with the kind of resigned wryness that comes from decades of fighting for a stability just out of reach. *I've been through so much trauma and financial stress that things don't even phase me*, she often thinks. *There are only two things that matter to me: Can we eat and do we have a place to live? Those are my priorities. I've had so many credit cards, but at the end of the day, if I have to pay VISA or rent, y'all gonna have to just sell it in collections. My credit is shot.*

Colissa was raised in Far Rockaway to parents who have been married for some fifty-odd years. Her mother worked as a receptionist in New York City's vast hospital network answering calls that came in to the hospital. Her father worked in reinsurance on Wall Street where he handled big accounts. The couple faced discriminatory redlining while trying to purchase a home in a better neighborhood, but they eventually found a nice home in Queens on a dead-end street where they raised Colissa. And yet, Colissa has found it impossible to replicate the middle-class stability her parents achieved.

Colissa graduated from Jamaica High School and got her teacher's certification at Hunter College. Since then, she's never struggled to find work. She worked as a police officer, until she became a single mother, and the hours as a post-9/11 NYPD cop became too difficult. She has also worked for a domestic violence agency and has run a family shelter. But her default is teaching. Teachers can always find work. Whether they can live on their wages is a whole other story.

Colissa has two daughters, one nine years old and one twenty-five years old. Things took a turn for the worse when the father of her second child threw them out. *He got upset and he was like, "Get out," but he didn't say it that nice. So I had a friend come pick me up and take me to a shelter that accepts families, and I got placed in a hotel. We were there some months until I came up with my Georgia plan.*

This was the Georgia plan: the father of Colissa's older daughter had passed away, and she had access to his death benefits. She knew they wouldn't get her very far in New York but thought she could make it stretch further somewhere cheaper until she got on her feet. Her father was from Augusta, so she had ties there—not a lot, but a friend and a few family members—so she picked herself up and moved to Georgia.

Colissa applied for food stamps and Medicaid for her daughter and moved into a shelter in Athens. She found work easily as a substitute teacher making $125 a day, and because she was in the shelter and didn't have to pay rent, she was able to put a bit away. She pulled together some money, and with some help from the shelter, she was able to put down a deposit for an apartment. She continued subbing for a year, and then the shelter she had stayed at asked her if she would run it, so she was hired as shelter director. It was a position that required a social-work degree, which Colissa didn't have, but they were impressed with her, and figured she'd been through the program, she knew it as well as anyone else. She worked there for a couple of years, but things got tense when the director of the organization accused her of taking a check that had come in late from a provider. Colissa didn't like that. He'd known her for years—how could he accuse her of stealing? So she left and found her way back to teaching.

She got a job at an alternative school that serves kids who are kicked out of all the other schools—ex-offenders, gang members, that kind of kid. She's always worked at inner-city schools, so she had the experience. Around that time, Colissa was granted custody of her grandkids. Her older daughter doesn't always make the best choices, and she was arrested for child endangerment because she was driving Colissa's grandkids without a car seat, plus her boyfriend had drug paraphernalia in the car, so the kids ended up with Colissa. She's now taking care of her two daughters and her two grandkids.

Colissa had hoped to get married like her parents—had even dreamed of being a stay-at-home mom. But her life didn't turn out that way. She was raised very religious and could not see herself ever getting an abortion, though she is outraged at the idea of that decision being taken away from women who have to suffer the consequences. Colissa is a registered independent—*I vote for the best candidate*—and her views on political issues are complex.

But Colissa is not an outlier in not being able to reproduce the middle-class stability she grew up with. Seven out of ten Black children born into the middle class will fall into the bottom by the time they are grown, while half of Black children born into poverty will stay poor. Meanwhile, most Black families with children are headed by a single parent.[2]

When I envisioned my life, I certainly envisioned my life with someone that we had that binding agreement and we were going to do this life together, but I just never got married. The father of the twenty-five-year-old was an alcoholic, and he became abusive at one time, and that was it for me, because you're not gonna put your hands on me. Then I was single for a long time because I had a little girl, and I was afraid that somebody was gonna do something to her, so I didn't enter another relationship for fifteen years. And the relationship that I entered was with the youngest daughter's father, who obviously had issues because he put us out on the street—matter of fact, more than one time. When he got angry, he would just put us out. So it would be my hope that I would've found somebody sound enough that was willing to help me carry the burden. That's what my parents modeled, even though it wasn't easy for them. I wish I would get married, but it just hasn't been in the cards for me yet. My theory is that mothers raise their daughters and love their sons, so the men that I encounter, I feel like they want a mother rather than a partner.

And there's no difference between men in New York and men in Georgia. *Men are the same everywhere.* Colissa does believe that the problem is worse in the Black community, though.

This introduction of public assistance—I know it was designed for elders and for people that couldn't work. But currently, that's not necessarily a clear description of who receives these services. And I feel that the introduction of those things, coupled with the requirement that there was no man in the home, really did a lot to break down the Black family structure. And if we can go back even further, we can look at the institution of slavery where men were used to breed children and families were ripped apart. So I think that some of these things are in our emotional DNA. I'm not saying that white women don't conceive without being married, but in my mind, my perception is such that it's more of an issue in the Black community because of those two reasons. The generation before me, there were different values. Now I feel like receiving those services to some degree is glorified. You hear it in rap songs. People talk about their EBT card and it's no big deal, so when I receive those services, I don't have that same level of shame that my mother may have had going to the store with food stamps. But to me, I've been working since I was fourteen, so if I get into a spot where I am not able to survive, I feel like it is my right having paid taxes to use those services temporarily for the purpose for which they were intended—until I get on my feet.

It's proving hard. Colissa is struggling, though she works full time at a middle school. She makes $48,000 a year, even though the job requires much more than eight hours a day of work. Her rent is $1,900 a month, and she's feeding a household of five. She gets some money from the government for the grandchildren in her custody, and she gets child support from her younger daughter's father, but it's never enough to cover all the bills. Three-quarters of her paycheck goes to rent, which means she can't pay it with a single paycheck and has to split it up into two payments. Her car was recently repossessed. She always has to call the electric company to defer payment and pay the bill over time, but even so, sometimes the electricity gets shut off.

The American Dream is a lie. Not a lie—let me backtrack. It feels like a lie, because not everyone can attain it. I'm as American as they come, but I can't get it. The American Dream to me is a house, a two-car garage, the ability to go on vacation, and pay for college. Perhaps if I were married and had the comfort of two incomes, if I weren't the main wage earner or head of household, maybe it would be a little more attainable, but not on a teacher's salary as a single individual with children to support. I've just accepted that and try to make the best of life.

What would help? *A raise and a credit reset, and some job protection. To be paid what I'm worth—that's all I'm asking—for my years of experience. Don't get me wrong: If I'm in a position where I need somebody to give me something, I'll take it. But if I have the capacity to work for it, I would rather be compensated for my work than just handed something. That's part of how I was raised. It's my fabric and my pride.*

———

Corrie, too, is struggling. A thirty-seven-year-old married mother of three—a sixteen-year-old, a thirteen-year-old, and a nine-year-old—her economic situation is dire. Her family is currently homeless; they are living with her sister, her brother-in-law, and her two nieces, so it's nine of them crunched into a tiny two-bedroom, one-bathroom house. *You can imagine, all those people in such a small space, it's not good.*

Corrie and her family ended up at her sister's owing to a perfect storm of circumstances: They had to move from their last place because the landlord was terrible, and Corrie lost her job just as they were transitioning. Corrie's husband, a quality-assurance auditor, had also recently changed jobs and taken a pay cut to reduce his commute time and stress levels by half. The plan had been to stay with her sister for a month, max. But now it's been six months and they have no prospects for moving out.

It's been very hard finding someone to rent to them, because both Corrie and her husband have bad credit—primarily thanks to medical bills from a couple of visits to the ER that they had to put on credit cards out of desperation. *No one wants to rent to someone with bad credit. Even when we tell them we're homeless, it doesn't matter. People don't understand what it means to be homeless. We're conditioned to think of homeless people as people living out of their cars, but before we came to my sister, we were living in a hotel.*

There are a lot of families struggling like Corrie's—employed, working hard, or looking for work, with nowhere to live.

Corrie grew up in Mason, Ohio. Her parents got divorced when she was pretty young. Her dad worked for the same company for twenty-seven years, in fleet management at a car dealership. Growing up, Corrie wouldn't say they were poor, but they definitely were not middle class. *I always had what I needed, and very little of what I wanted.* Corrie graduated from high school, with the last two years of high school doubling as technical school in health-information management. She went to college right after, but it didn't work out. She was burned out from high school, didn't have the best grades, and didn't know what she wanted to do. *It was that stupid lie we all got told, us older millennials when we were in school—"You have to go to college straight out of high school." I went to college because that's what I thought I was supposed to do, rather than because it was something I really wanted to do.*

So she dropped out and began a series of jobs that didn't require a college degree. She worked on and off for McDonald's for many years, which was a good first job, though she never wanted to make a career out of it. She worked at an amusement park for four years, then went back to McDonald's, and she did a few stints in direct care working for a friend who has two disabled daughters. At some point, she decided that medical transcription seemed practical, so she did a course in adult education when her children were young, but by the time she finished the training, the field had disappeared thanks to the invention of speech to text technology. So she became a stay-at-home mom for five years when her kids were little, and then she got the job at the Children's Hospital. She was there for a year until the commute got to her. Currently she's working part time as a scheduler in a gastroenterology office.

Corrie and her family are in a predicament known to many working-class Americans. They are stuck between a rock and a hard place: they make too much to qualify for government assistance, but not enough to ensure any security or quality of life for their family, and even finding a home to rent has become almost impossible because of their bad credit. The cheapest rent Corrie could find was $900 a month for a three-bedroom, but to get a lease, she needs to be able to show she and her husband are making three times the rent, which would be $2,700—more than she and her husband bring in.

Corrie understands that landlords need good tenants. But so much of the application process now happens online that she doesn't even get to make a case for her family. They are being rejected out-of-hand because of their credit, or because they don't make enough money. But fixing her credit feels impossible: you can't apply for too many credit cards or it dings your credit score, and she doesn't have the kind of monthly bills that help improve it because she's homeless.

Corrie firmly believes housing should be guaranteed no matter what for everyone in the country. *For us to have a functioning society, for people to be able to live and do what they need to do to take care of themselves and their families, they shouldn't have to worry about housing. People abusing the system and abusing government help are very few and far between. They're out there, but I don't think they're as common as people like to think they are.*

What is common is hardworking families who have fallen on hard times and have no one to help them. Even if Corrie and her husband qualified for government assistance, the Section 8 waiting list is two years long. By then, Corrie is hoping to have solved her problems, at least the major one of not having a place to live. She just needs a temporary assist, a hand up. She doesn't want to go to a shelter because she thinks it would be traumatizing for her kids. But even if she did want to go to a shelter, the ones in her area are all full.

Living with her sister has been hard on the family, especially her nine-year-old. He has special needs and a lot of emotional issues and anger problems, and Corrie's sister has a nine-year-old girl who's just three months younger than him. Both are very headstrong, and while some days they do great together, there are days when they fight and fight, and that puts stress on everyone else.

To Corrie, the American Dream means being able to live in a house that she owns. *I don't need to be super rich or anything like that. I just need to be able to live comfortably without having to struggle all the time for things. I want to be able to have everything that I need and that my kids need and be able to give them some things that they want, maybe take a vacation every once in a while with all the kids and be able to do that without having to struggle and worry about where am I going to have to pull money from in order to make this happen? Or am I gonna have to give up some food in the house in order to do this? I just want to be able to live comfortably and independently and not have to worry about any government assistance, not have to worry about asking family and friends for money when I can't afford things. That's what I want. That's my goal.*

She fervently believes it's achievable—if only she and her husband were able to pull in the median household income in the U.S., somewhere between $60,000 and $70,000 a year. If Corrie could just get their combined incomes into that range, she'd have everything she needed.

She thinks she'll get there—but it will be a struggle. *I believe the American Dream exists for immigrants to this country, but for Americans themselves, I don't think it really exists much anymore. It seems much easier for someone who comes into the country to get access to the resources needed to build whatever it is they're trying to build. But it seems like for average Americans to get access to those resources is 10,000 times harder than it would be for someone else. I wish I knew why. I believe people can really achieve what they put their minds to. But it just seems like it's been my experience that the people who try the hardest seem to have the toughest time getting the things that they need.*

What Corrie needs most is just someone to give her a chance. *We need a break somehow, some way. That's really it. If we could just find someone willing to work with us instead of against us, that would be nice.*

We'll get there. I know we'll get there. It's just a matter of things falling into place and getting the things that we need to make it happen. I don't want to be given everything, you know? I want to have some sense of pride in working for what I have, but it's just … it would be nice if things could be made a bit easier, that's all.

———

Kevin Nelson works in janitorial services. He lives in Anaheim, California. He is tall and thin with dark skin and black hair, and at forty-six, he has a seriousness about him that is softened by the carefully protected hope in his eyes. Kevin grew up in Compton, where money was tight. There was just enough for the basic necessities, but no matter how little the family had, Kevin's parents helped others. *We always had enough, or they made sure it was enough to share with other people around us—family, neighbors, just all kinds of different people. Regardless of what we had going on, they helped.*

Kevin's mother was a certified nurse's aide, and his father—

his stepfather actually; his real dad wasn't around—was a social worker who focused on gang intervention, which kept him busy in Compton. The gang culture was there right outside the house, and sometimes closer. Cousins and older friends in the neighborhood would routinely get sucked in. *I did hang with people, and sometimes I got in trouble—never too much trouble, but little scrapes here and there, and then I just started realizing like, Hey, this isn't it. I got older cousins, older friends, and I saw where that lifestyle was taking them. People were getting killed. I knew I didn't want that at an early age. I didn't want that to be my story.*

Kevin believes that the fact that he had a father and mother at home acted like a magnetic pull away from irreversible mistakes. It gave him an alternative to strive for, but also a sense of accountability. *I was the only person who had a two-parent household. Everybody else I knew stayed with their mother, their grandmother, or a variation of somebody in their family. But none of my friends came from a household where they had a mom and a dad. I was the only person. And I knew that no matter what I did with my friends, if I went too far outside the line, I would have to deal with my father when I came home. And because he's a social worker, everybody kind of knows him, so I knew it would get back to him. That figurehead really stopped me from doing a lot of things because I just didn't want to have to deal with my father. He would tell us about different people—"Watch how this person turned out and you watch how this turns out." He gave us knowledge on why a lot of people around us would go down the wrong road. It was because they didn't have a role model. There wasn't somebody to tell them no.*

Kevin joined the military at eighteen, and it was a great experience. The satisfaction of serving his country was a big deal for him, but he also learned responsibility, how to manage a team, and that you need to pay attention and keep your head focused or someone gets hurt. When Kevin was twenty, he had his first son, and after three years, the child's mother dropped him at Kevin's door and took off, which made him a single dad. His mom helped, but she was very clear that he was going to have to raise his own son. She wasn't going to be like the other grandmothers in Compton. So Kevin stepped up. *My lifestyle just changed overnight. I was still young, I'm out partying, doing what young people do. And then when he came to stay with me, overnight, I had to hit the brakes on that.*

He left the military after four years and started a series of jobs—supervisor work, warehouse work, power washing, painting. He had another child who turned out to have autism and will never be able to live independently, which means Kevin and the child's mother take turns taking care of him. That was hard for Kevin to accept—that he couldn't will his son to have a better life. His oldest is now twenty-five, and his second son is eighteen, and then he had two little babies, seven and five, and they brighten up his life.

But he's no longer with their mother—in large part thanks to work stress. Kevin started his own cleaning company, Quality Cleaning Solutions, during the COVID lockdowns. Someone he knew made an offhand remark about how there was going to be millionaires and billionaires made out of the pandemic, and a lightbulb went off in Kevin's head. Then he found out what government contracts were paying for cleaning services, and that sealed the deal: they were paying real money. So Kevin started looking into cleaning, studying it, coming up with a value-add. He learned about COVID spraying and bringing a heat element to his cleaning, and he learned how to do COVID fogging and started getting cleaning jobs.

Kevin has always been something of a dreamer. *Why not me? Why can't I have a big company and achieve these big goals? I could tell you that the color of my skin makes my world harder, okay? I could waste time complaining about it. But the greatest thing about being here in this country—you could talk about everything bad about it, but the one thing that we do have is hard work. Perseverance can get you somewhere. It can literally get you somewhere. I am the poster child of that.*

Hard work—and prayer—are the keys to success, Kevin believes. And he finds deep peace in the work. When he gets cleaning, he zones out and finds an inner sense of calm. He loves the way he feels after a hard day's work. He loves the feeling of accomplishment. *For whatever reason, I just love getting my hands dirty. It gets my juices going. I just love the work part of it.*

But sometimes even that is not enough. The good paying government contracts take a long time to pay. Sometimes you're chasing people down for months, trying to get them to pay you what they owe. Government workers leave and suddenly there's a new director, and you have to start trying to get your money all over again with someone new. And getting business is hard, competing with cleaning companies that employ illegal immigrants, who will work for $10, $11 an hour. Kevin isn't even comfortable paying people minimum wage; he insists on paying people enough so that they will be able to pay their bills after a long, hard day of work. He feels sick at the idea of someone paying 30 percent of his check just on gas to get to work. *A lot of that is me thinking back to when I was there, I gave this grand effort, and when I get my check, I can't pay my bills.* He tries to only take contracts that let him pay workers $30–$35 an hour.

He has been able to hire people from back in Compton, give them a shot at something. But he does a lot of the cleaning himself. *If you want me to be honest, as far as cleaning goes—industrial cleaning, janitor cleaning—I don't think nobody's better than me. I found something. Everybody has something. Some people never find it, some people do. I found my thing. And it took me forty years to find it, but I found it. That's how you get the American Dream. The main thing is: Work hard. Work hard.*

But it can be too much hard work. Kevin's relationship suffered as a result of his commitment to his business, and he's alone now. He had a partner in his business for a while—Kevin Harper, a friend he met back in the military—but he, too, stepped back when he felt the business was encroaching on his family life. Kevin has struggled to find workers who will put in the dedication he does to the cleaning. And though he's been at it a few years, Kevin still feels like he's living in poverty.

I'm somewhere between poverty and working class. There are months where money is very, very tight. He doesn't own a home and he has no savings, and whatever he has he's poured into his business. He is living on a knife-edge, with all the people he has to support. *My reality is I'm a check away from being . . . certain things. But you'll never hear me speak like that. Because of the determination.*

He is determined to make his American Dream come true. He wants to be an inspiration to the people around him. He longs to be an example of how hard work pays off, to inspire and to become someone known for giving back to the community like his parents were.

I won't give up. The fight is hard, but I don't have quit in me. I don't want to fail at what I'm doing. I have belief that eventually, something will come along and give me a push into another stratosphere. I still have opportunity, after everything I've been through in life, I still have an opportunity. Where else in the world can you come from nothing and then build yourself up to something? Me, I'm the American Dream. I have to work myself from the bottom floor up and keep building myself up. It's only a matter of time. I feel like I am destined to be really good at what I do.

———

Maria was raised by wolves. She was kicked out of her family home when she was fifteen, and from then on she had to raise herself. Her childhood had been abusive. She grew up in Pomona, California, and moved to Los Angeles after she got kicked out to live with one of her girlfriends.

Once in L.A., she was a real hustler. She had her own car, which she turned into her own personal cab service. She made people pay her to drive them places. She was sixteen years old. *You know, when you're desperate, you figure out different ways of making money, and that's how I did it.* She also got a job at CVS, which helped pay the bills.

When she was twenty-one, she married the father of her oldest daughter, but like her parents, he was abusive, so she left him and moved in with a family member until she got back on her feet. She was only married to her second husband for three months, but her third husband, the one she's with now, that was the real deal. That marriage has lasted twenty-six years.

Maria's husband works for General Motors, and when he got transferred to Reno, Nevada, Maria went with him, giving up the business she'd started helping lower-income people with bad credit become homeowners. She assumed she'd be able to start something similar in Reno, but her husband's mother developed Alzheimer's, and suddenly, Maria became a full-time caregiver.

Maria jokes that she's a caregiver not by choice, or rather, it chose her. But while it's a full-time job—365 days a year, twenty-four hours a day, seven days a week—Maria is paid for only twenty-five hours a week, at just $10 an hour. It's next to nothing, certainly not enough to cover her bills. But Maria can't get another job because if something happens with her mother-in-law, she needs to be available to her 24/7. *She goes to daycare. If she gets sick or if they don't show up to pick her up, I couldn't work a normal job because I always have to be available for her. I've tried to work a normal job and then I have to leave in the middle of the day because she got sick on herself or she's not feeling well, and they call me and tell me to come pick her up, or she pooped on herself. I'm at her beck and call, so I really can't work a normal job because I'm caring for her.*

But Maria would never consider putting her mother-in-law in a home. Her first job alongside CVS was working for an old-folks facility, and the way they treated the elderly turned her off for life. *I would never do that to someone I loved. And my mother-in-law isn't verbal, so she can't tell me if there's something wrong with her, if someone touched her, if someone abused her, if someone hit her. So I refuse to put her someplace where I feel like somebody could do something to her and I would not know about it. I'm fifty-six years old. I'm not a spring chicken anymore. But I still can't do it. I couldn't do it and live with myself.*

So instead Maria sacrificed her professional life to caring for her mother-in-law, and it's taking a big toll on the family. They are struggling. Her husband works ten to twelve hours a day, and sometimes she doesn't see him at all. He comes home, goes to bed, gets back up and goes to work.

Financially, we suck right now. Our bills are sky high, our credit cards are up to the limit. The couple owns a home, but it's uninhabitable because of flooding, so instead they are renting, but rent keeps jumping higher and higher. Maria has to call the electric company once a month and make arrangements and payment schedules because she can't afford to pay the bill. And she's still taking care of her kids, even though they are grown.

Still, Maria doesn't complain. She believes we make our own American Dream. *This is heaven right here. I'm happy because I have a good partner. I have everything that I want and I need for. I'm not hungry, I'm not lacking in anything. I have to just appreciate the little things, to where I can go outside and look at the beautiful green trees and feel the breeze and just say, Wow, what a beautiful day it is, look at what God gave us. Look at what we have right now on this earth and what we have to absorb. It took a lot of therapy. It took a lot of me getting to know myself and getting to be happy with myself.*

The hardest thing about having to give up her career for starvation wages is that Maria knows she would be financially successful if she had kept applying herself. *I would probably be a millionaire, a multimillionaire if I didn't have to stop what I was doing to care for my family. But, you know, life . . . it is, it is what it is, right? We make our choices in our lives, and my choice is to love my loved ones more than financial success.*

She is also enraged that after spending her life paying taxes to the government, her mother-in-law gets so little back in return. *Even though she spent her life providing for the state, paying her taxes, paying her property taxes, paying her taxes when she went into the grocery store and bought groceries, she is only allotted twenty-five hours a week. If it wasn't me taking care of her, nobody would be able to take care of her.*

Maria is a solid Democrat. She feels the Republicans always want what's best for the rich people. Democrats want what's best for the regular people. But she tries to stay out of politics because she doesn't want to get angry. What she does want is to be fairly compensated for her work, and to be able to provide care for her loved ones that doesn't impoverish her.

For now, those goals are out of reach. *If we can get to $15 or $16 an hour, that will make a difference.*

———

Oshrat lives in Rockville, Maryland. She's a single mom to a sixteen-year-old and a nine-year-old, and she doesn't get much help from her ex-husband, a couple hundred dollars now and again but not in any consistent way. She teaches Hebrew and drama in a Jewish school to third and fifth graders, and she makes $44,000 a year. Every month is a struggle, though some are definitely harder than others, like the summer and winter months when electricity and gas bills are higher. Somehow, she always manages to cover everything, though she often has to ask for help. And she has no savings. She has no idea how she will ever be able to afford to retire.

Unlike all the other single moms she knows, Oshrat was able to buy her home, something she considers a miracle. She had excellent credit and worked with a loan officer to secure a very low interest rate and down payment based on her income and her being the head of her household through a program that no longer exists. *I'm a very resourceful person. That's the only way I'm making it work. Otherwise, I would be deep in debt.* During the COVID lockdowns, she got some money from the government, which she saved up and then used throughout the following two years to tackle the kinds of extra bills that cropped up. She stretched the payments as much as she could.

She also credits her resourcefulness with how she managed to graduate from college without a lot of student loans, and what loans she had she's managed mostly to pay off. She studied computer science in college, but she enjoyed teaching more, plus she was able to spend more time with her kids that way. She knows she could get more money if she went back to computers, but she'd sacrifice being able to be there for her kids. *Everybody always says, well, go back to your old profession. You can make much more money. They're right, but it's much more of an investment. It means taking time away from my children. And I wasn't willing to give up on that. If they had somebody else besides me, that would be something else. But it's just me.*

Things would be much easier if she was still married because the burden would be divided. *On my own, just one person, it's a miracle that I manage to maintain my home and have food and everything.* There's the mortgage, which is $1,900 a month, and then electricity and water, plus the maintenance of the house. There are leaks or clogs, or the sewer backs up, the kinds of things that can be very challenging to budget for. She often has to ask for help for these sorts of expenses.

What Oshrat really needs is to make more money. She takes on tutoring when she can, but it's not something she can count on as a consistent income. But when she asked for a cost-of-living raise, she was turned down. Still, she doesn't feel she can leave to try to find something else, because she has a solid income coming in, and even though it's tight, it's a sure thing. *I have to stick to my job to make sure that the house is paid and the girls have whatever they need.*

Oshrat grew up middle class; her father was a military man who then started a business, and her mother was a paralegal. But today, she would call herself working class. She doesn't feel like she has the kind of stability that would qualify as a middle-class life, especially without a retirement plan, something she thinks about a lot. To her, the American Dream would mean being able to save for retirement, being able to take a nice vacation with her children once in a while, and being able to buy them new clothes. She relies on hand-me-downs for her younger daughter, and her sixteen-year-old buys her own clothes with her babysitting money. Oshrat wishes she could get them nice things. Her kids think she's cheap because she can't buy them things like Lululemon leggings.

Her youngest daughter mumbled something about how they were poor the other day, and that really struck her.

"We have everything we need," she told her daughter. "We have clothes, we have food, and you have to understand, I just have to make sure that whatever I'm making, it goes to where it needs to go first before I can even think of Lululemons or Nikes."

To be able to provide everything for everyone, that would be my American Dream: the lack of concern of how you make it the next month. I don't have that. I'm scratching at the American Dream. I have a white fence, but it's broken. With one income, it's really, really, really hard to make it. It's very, very challenging.

———

Nehemiah always wanted to be a nurse, but to become a nurse, you need to go to school. And to go to school, you need to pay for school. You need somewhere to live. You need some way to pay for food while you're not working. And Nehemiah doesn't have any of that.

He grew up in Durham, North Carolina, in the projects. What he remembers from his childhood is that the teachers were nice to him in elementary school because his mom had heart problems. Then she passed away when he was eight, leaving him and his sister with a stepfather who drank. There aren't a lot of good memories after that.

Nehemiah did start taking classes at Durham Tech Community College, but after a blowout fight with his stepfather, he had to find somewhere else to live, which meant finding a job, which meant leaving school. That's how he ended up working the grill at McDonald's, becoming one of America's 3.4 million fast-food workers. It's one of the growing industries in the U.S. and pays a median wage of $25,000 a year. After rent in even some of the cheapest places to live in the U.S., that leaves barely anything at all. And yet, millions and millions of hardworking Americans toil at these jobs, somehow making it work. People like Nehemiah.

Nehemiah works the grill, which means he knows how to prepare all the McDonald's menu items. There's the nuggets, which have a timer. You drop them in the grease, press the button on the timer, and after three minutes max, you pull them out, drain the grease, and put them in a tray. There's the Big Mac: put the bread in the toaster, put the patty on the grill, put on the lettuce, tomato, onions, then another burger, then another patty on top. The patties are frozen when they go on the grill, and you're supposed to add salt and pepper, but Nehemiah noticed that it dries the patties out. He stopped eating Big Macs after that, even though they are free for employees on shift.

Nehemiah doesn't mind working at McDonald's. It all depends on the vibe, though. Sometimes the vibe is good. Sometimes the vibe is bad. Then it can get real bad.

You know right away when you walk in what the vibe is. When the vibe is bad, you don't take your headphones off until you're by your locker putting everything away to get ready for your shift. You keep those headphones on until the last possible minute. That's one way of coping.

You put your stuff away and head straight to the grill. By then, the vibe is undeniable, especially because the grill staff talks the most. They have to communicate about the food, but of course, it goes way beyond that, especially if a manager talks to an employee in a way they don't like. That's how drama starts. By the night shift on a bad day, the bad vibes have turned thick, like humidity. The night shift is definitely the most dramafied. Nehemiah avoids the night shift.

But the vibe isn't just created by the other members of the staff. It's a joint creation of staff and customers, a kind of grand production where each side is supposed to hold its own but the weakest link in either chain can have a snowball effect. Like if a customer comes up to the window and starts asking for things this way and that way, they want it special to order and whatnot, Nehemiah will say, "Sure, no problem," but as soon as he rings them up, they catch an attitude and start cursing him out. So he gets mad. Sometimes staff will curse them back and then managers will get up on them, "Don't talk to customers like that." That's gonna start drama for sure.

It's really about getting along with your manager, getting along with your coworkers, and getting along with the customers. If you can get along with all three, you'll have a good shift.

There are three kinds of customers who come into McDonald's, Nehemiah has noticed. There are cool customers, the dailies who know what they want before they get there, they know what the price is, they know who's working. They'll come in and order a Mac Double, no onions, no pickle, vanilla milkshake and a small fry, or they'll order a Mac Chicken and a small fry and a Hawaiian fruit punch.

Then you have what Nehemiah and his coworkers call the "ghetto" customers who come in, *I want this, I want that. My stuff better be done this way, my stuff better be done that way.* That's the kind of person who makes the whole vibe turn from good to bad.

Then you have the sightseers, people who are just giving McDonald's a shot for the first time. They will often wait two weeks and then come back. Then they become dailies.

Nehemiah's philosophy is, he will respect anyone to a certain extent, but if they're arguing just for the sake of arguing, he's not cool with that.

He comes in most days at 2:00 p.m. and leaves around 11:00. He started at $7.95 an hour but the company raised their wages to $9.75 in 2020. He's living with his stepmom and his brother, and they share the cost of rent and groceries. Rent is $500 a month, so that comes to around $200 apiece, and after $100 for groceries, that leaves just about $100, and usually he spends that on food, too; he gets hungry on the way to work, or on the way home. Which means there's really nothing left over for college. Or for anything else.

That's what working at McDonald's means, at the end of the day: a lot of hard choices about what you spend your money on. Or maybe, not many choices at all.

———

Lucia works at a Family Dollar store in Brooklyn. She's been there just over a year. Prior to that she helped out with her god-daughter who was born premature, a job she took after she was laid off at the BJ's liquor store. Her partner works for the state as a regional supervisor over the streets, so he rents a house up in

Albany and lives there most of the time. Lucia lives in New York City public housing with their fourteen-year-old daughter and twenty-five-year-old son. Her thirty-year-old son is a regional manager at a BJs in New Jersey and has moved out. Her twenty-five-year-old also works at BJ's, the overnight shift, but he's not quite ready to leave her.

For a family of four like Lucia's, the New York City Housing Authority's upper limit on income is $113,000 a year. But Lucia is not in danger of exceeding it. She only gets twenty-five hours a week at Family Dollar, where she makes $15.50 an hour; there's no full-time unless you're in management. But Lucia is patient; she knows if she works hard, she'll rise up the ladder. It's happened so many times before. She usually brings in about $1,200 a month, and the way the public housing works is she pays them a third of her income, whatever she's making. Right now that's between $300 and $400. The rest goes to groceries and other necessities for the house. When she was working at BJ's full time, her rent was much higher; she was paying $1,055 a month, which the housing authority dropped when she lost that job.

She could never afford to live in Brooklyn if she had to pay rent. It's why her second son doesn't move out; he can't, either, though he's very generous with her, "You sure you don't need anything?" especially when he wants her to cook for him. The cheapest one-bedroom these days goes for what she makes in a month. She feels lucky to have her apartment, though the area has gotten rougher since she moved in twenty years ago. It used to be that her housing complex was mostly the elderly. Now it's a mix of city workers, people who work for the subway and make $40,000 a year, and a younger element that Lucia doesn't approve of. It's still a nice development, but there's more crime than there ever was before. But she doesn't think she can afford to move, even to join her husband in Albany. The public housing apartment anchors her to the neighborhood, in a way that's both good and bad.

She worked at BJ's for about three years. She applied for and got a job as a cashier, full-time. Then they asked her to work in HR. Then they wanted her to be management, so she said yes, but as soon as she was trained, BJ's killed the position and she got severance and was out of a job. *Y'all could have just left me where I was. I didn't even ask for the position.*

But Lucia knew she'd find something else. She's been working since she was thirteen and her mom got sick and her dad, an alcoholic, walked out, and the state was giving her mom just $300 a month for disability and there were two mortgages to pay. The family had been middle class; Lucia's mom was a nurse and her dad worked in the animal lab at the Brooklyn Jewish Hospital, but they started a quick descent with her mother's illness.

Her first job was as a waitress; it remains the best job she has ever had. She made $2.95 an hour plus tips, and it was the only job she ever had that you could show up at flat broke and come home with a pocketful of cash. You met people, you had conversations, but it wasn't like today; cranky customers were few and far between. Her son was a baby, and her husband would watch him in the morning and her mother would take over in the evening until she came home from work.

Then her mother passed at just forty-eight after a battle with kidney failure and a rejected transplant, and Lucia was on her own. She worked for ten years at a bank, starting as a teller and working her way up to manager, but the bank closed in 2008, and since then it's been cashier jobs for the most part. At Family Dollar she's a cashier, but she also stocks shelves and puts items back, wherever she can be useful. She works part-time Sunday through Wednesday, then usually gets Thursday off, then comes back Friday and Saturday.

Lucia takes pride in her work, whatever she's doing. She's not one to lollygag and drag her feet. She treats every job like a million-dollar job, like she's getting a million-dollar paycheck every week. That's how her parents raised her. Be grateful for any job because you might not have it. It's a blessing.

She now calls herself working class; there's no middle anymore, and she's definitely not at the bottom. If she was given the choice to not work and get more benefits, or to work for more money, she would take the better job, hands down, with no hesitation. The few times she's had to ask for help, when times got hard and she lost her job, she didn't like how it made her feel. And it was *her* money, too—she'd paid that unemployment insurance.

She was raised by parents who worked hard, even when there was trouble. Her mom wasn't one of those moms who said, "Oh, you're not feeling good? Stay home from school." And she's the same. Her children have perfect attendance. That's a big deal for her. She's always worked and she always will work. She's paid out enough into social security to collect, but she doesn't think she'll retire anytime soon. A coworker told her recently that he couldn't afford to retire, and she thought, *Wow, that's true for me, too. You work until you can't work no more. And now it seems you gotta work 'til you lease out.*

Lucia is fiercely independent. She wouldn't want to move out of her apartment and move in with her partner unless she knew she could afford to pay the rent herself. You never know what's going to happen. And she tells her kids the same thing: *If you wanna move in with somebody, make sure that you can pay that entire rent yourself. Because what if they leave?*

Even paying what she owes the public housing authority is a challenge on what she's bringing in these days. Sometimes she doesn't have $500 at a time in one paycheck, so she sends in $150, $200 as it comes in. *You make it happen. You do what you have to do.*

Lucia doesn't feel financially stable. She's been let go of jobs that liked her and liked her work too many times to feel like just working hard and giving 100 percent is enough. At any point, they can turn around and say, Hey, we're making cuts, so nothing is really stable. She knows she's a good worker, even though sometimes she's late. But she also knows companies cut costs all the time, especially the kinds of companies that hire at her skill level.

When it comes to politics, Lucia thinks all politicians are full of garbage. She doesn't like any party more than the other. *I don't believe them, whether it's Democrat or Republican, because they all talk the same game to get in there. They get us all to believe the hype. But then the reality is—and I always try to think positive, I don't think they wanted to go in here and not do it, I truly think maybe that they did plan to, but then I feel like there's so much corruption.*

Lucia is especially frustrated about immigration. *Everybody is running here to achieve the American Dream. And I just feel like, how can you promise this to other people when you can't even take care of ones that you have here? We have homelessness, we have crime, we have poverty. And yet we keep bringing more. And don't get me wrong: they deserve that freedom or whatever dream that they want to have here. But it's like my mother always said: Don't go sticking your nose in nobody else's backyard when your backyard is not clean. We can't clean our own backyard. How do we help others? We have veterans who risked their lives who are homeless. Why is that? Why do we have homeless veterans on the street in this country? They stood on the front line for our freedom and we can't feed them, we can't house them, but yet we'll bring other people and feed them. And then they don't understand why people are angry.*

For Lucia, the American Dream means being able to pay her rent and not having to worry, not having to rob Peter to pay Paul, not having to choose which bills to pay and which to have to hold off on and pay late fees on. Maybe a family vacation now and again, if your kids are into it. *Everybody's dream is different, but a lot of people come to the United States to be able to have that kind of stability, but the way it's being done now is making the people who are already here miserable. I don't want to be rich. With money comes obligations and problems. I just want to be comfortable. Stable. I don't want to have to worry am I going to be able to pay basic bills, am I going to get let go tomorrow. The American Dream is just being able to live without that fear of, you know, are we going to be out of food? Do we have to make that choice between groceries and rent? Do I have to make that choice these days? Always. Always.*

CHAPTER 2

FLOATING

Setting out to get an accurate portrait of the American working class is no easy feat, in large part because of how difficult it is to define "working class" and how diverse whatever group you end up with will be. One proxy for "working class" would be Americans making between $20,000 and $80,000 a year. Bear in mind that 15 percent of this group has a bachelor's degree. Now consider that 43 percent of the American labor force is in this category. That includes a third of our country—ninety-seven million Americans.

Of course, there is a world of difference between $20,000 a year and $80,000 a year. There are many parts of the country where $80,000 a year is a solidly middle-class income, and parts of the country where people who make more than $100,000 a year qualify for public housing. Any analysis of the American working class that aims to understand whether they have a fair shot at the American Dream is going to have to take geography into account.

If homeownership is the main factor in defining a middle-class life and the American Dream, the homeownership rate of Americans making $20,000–$80,000 a year by state tells us a lot about which states offer working-class Americans the best shot at the American Dream. Unfortunately, across the country, the rate of homeownership for the working class is falling.

In 2000, on a national level, the homeownership rate of Americans making between $20,000 and $80,000 a year was 69 percent. States like Alabama, Idaho, Indiana, Iowa, Kentucky, and Maine all had homeownership rates of more than 80 percent for working-class people defined in this way back then. Even in New York the rate was 63 percent.

Unfortunately, in the intervening twenty years, the share of working-class homeowners has fallen by a lot, to about 60 percent overall, and no state cracked the 80 percent homeownership rate for working-class Americans in 2021, although it was in the seventies for many states.

Ironically, working-class Americans are making more money than they have in a long time. Compare the breakdown in wages between 2000 and 2021, as shown in figure 7:

Figure 7. Wages in 2000 Compared to 2021.

PROPORTION OF MIDDLE CLASS IN INCOME RANGES, 2000		PROPORTION OF MIDDLE CLASS IN INCOME RANGES, 2021	
$20,000–$30,000	19.67%	$20,000–$30,000	15.34%
$30,000–$40,000	18.41%	$30,000–$40,000	15.18%
$40,000–$50,000	17.12%	$40,000–$50,000	15.52%
$50,000–$60,000	14.92%	$50,000–$60,000	15.06%
$60,000–$70,000	12.83%	$60,000–$70,000	14.74%
$70,000–$80,000	10.00%	$70,000–$80,000	13.82%

From the American Community Survey, 2020, prepared by Dr. Joe Price, Katherine Wilson, and Megan McQueen at Brigham Young University.

As you can see by comparing the two tables side by side, at least 9 percent of those making $20,000–$40,000 in 2000 are now making at least $60,000–$80,000. Overall, the share of the labor force making $20,000–$80,000 is 12 percent smaller now than it was in 2000, as you can see in figure 8.

Yet while some workers have dropped out of the labor force entirely, others have migrated even further up, into the top quintile.

Working-class Americans find themselves in a Catch-22: while they are making more money than twenty years ago, homeown-

Figure 8. Wages in 2000 Compared to 2021.

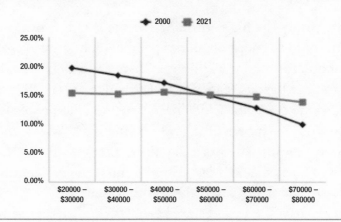

From the American Community Survey, 2020, prepared by Dr. Joe Price, Katherine Wilson, and Megan McQueen at Brigham Young University

ership is still out of reach because of skyrocketing home prices. More than 80 percent of Americans are making at least $16 an hour, yet the hallmarks of a middle-class life are increasingly beyond their means, however frugally they live and however hard they work. There are millions and millions of Americans who are hardworking and deeply committed to their jobs who will never be able to afford to retire, who have no savings and no ability to save due to the costs of housing and health care.

Amy is one of them. Amy is a certified nurse's aide (CNA) who works at a nursing home in South Florida. She's been at her job for thirty-three years. After her twentieth year, the company she works for put a up a plaque for her and gave her a parking spot, but a hurricane blew away the plaque.

Amy has a perfect, gray mullet and a smoker's laugh, though she's trying to quit smoking. I spent time with Amy during a heat wave in Florida during the day between her shifts. She was dressed in shorts, a T-shirt, and rainbow-colored crocs. While on duty, Amy usually wears white crocs to match her starched white uniform, the same every day. It's one more way she can convey a sense of calm and routine to the often-confused seniors in her care.

Amy works the night shift. When she gets to work, she goes room to room to check on all her people, make sure everybody's there and accounted for and safe. Then she gets her clean linen ready and her barrels ready for all the soiled sheets. Throughout the night, she does vitals and checks, turning her people to make sure they don't get bedsores, and if someone is awake and has a hard time sleeping, she sits and talks to them if she has the time. In the morning, she does last rounds, and if the patients are able, she dresses them and helps them into a chair.

Amy is fifty-seven, and she's been with her partner, Janet, also a CNA, for nineteen years. They live in a small house on Janet's mom's property and pay her $700 a month. It's an old house, built in 1943, with two bedrooms and one bath, but it's never just Amy and Janet. They are the kind of couple who takes in strays. They have three rescue dogs, and Janet's granddaughter is living with them. And for a long time, Amy's nephew Ryan lived with them after his mom lost custody of him. Ryan was diagnosed with autism and qualified for social security but he chose to give up his benefits and got a job at Amy's nursing home in the kitchen. He doesn't want to live off the government, and Amy is real proud of that. He wants to be in society. He wants to be like everybody else, go to community college, become a mechanic or start a business. When they are together, Amy insists he make eye contact because she knows that's important. She also knows it's hard for him.

Both Amy and Janet work two jobs, and Amy is interviewing for a third. They both have a main job with a nursing home but have taken on "private-duty" cases to help make car payments and medical expenses. Amy and Janet together usually manage to save about $3,000 every year, but the entirety of those savings end up going to medical expenses. Amy's deductible is $3,500, which means that she's got to have that in hand for anything that comes up, and something always comes up. She had a torn meniscus last year that had to be repaired, and that was $3,500 right there. It depleted their savings to $300, which means Janet is putting off taking care of her medical issues. She has a diabetic toe that's looking worse and worse. Amy is just hoping she doesn't get hurt and have to go on disability before she stops working.

Amy makes $22 an hour. It's the most she's ever made, but it's not enough to make her feel secure, and it's definitely not enough to save for retirement or get a mortgage. Amy can't imagine what will happen when her body can't handle the physical demands of her job anymore. Nobody she knows can. When Amy's union went to contract negotiations eight years ago with her company, a retirement plan was on the list, but the corporate lawyer they met with—his name was Bob—the first thing out of his mouth was, "I see you got retirement on here, and if you guys want to continue to discuss that, we're done right here, right now."

Amy's the union delegate of her shop, an elected position that means she liaises between management and the other workers. Whenever she can, she puts things to a vote. Then she takes that vote to the administrator and tells her what the workers want, and she tells Amy yay or nay. Mostly it's no. On big issues, Amy goes back to the members and they put together a delegation, sign a petition, make it official, and take it back to the administrator, explaining that the petition represents what the staff feels is best to take care of the residents.

A little while ago, Amy had a huge victory: she got the starting pay from $10.40 an hour to $18.35. But now the temp agencies are paying $22–$24 an hour, which is making it almost impossible to retain workers. The nursing home has just twelve CNAs, when it should have closer to fifty. A lot of people left to join temp agencies that hire out by the day and pay three or four more dollars an hour. Of course, Amy doesn't blame them.

When Amy first started at the nursing home, it was owned by an awesome company. They treated the workers really well and gave them all kinds of perks. But since then, it's been sold at least three times, and each time, things get worse. Now there's a management company that runs the facility for the corporation that owns it, and all they care about is making profit for the investors. *All they want is a return on that money. They cut and cut and cut the budget, until they are feeding the residents on a dollar a day. Imagine the food that that is.*

As the union delegate, Amy fights for better wages but also for safer and fairer working conditions. She's fighting to lower the ratio of CNAs to patients. Currently, it's twenty to one, which means patients don't get the care they need. And she's fighting against the company bringing in new hires and paying them more than the folks who have already been there, something they do all the time. And she's trying to get the cleaning staff's wages from $12.50 an hour to $13.50 an hour. She's real hopeful about that one.

Still, Amy doesn't think all jobs need unions. Some jobs are good jobs even without a union. But her job definitely needs that protection. It took her a while to realize that. Initially, she hadn't known much about unions. But then a friend of hers, Denise, a really sweet CNA, was accused by a resident of hurting her, and Denise was fired. Amy was 100 percent sure that the resident was mistaken—a common enough occurrence when you're dealing with Alzheimer's patients. She knew that Denise could never hurt anyone. But after a two-hour investigation, Denise was terminated. And then something miraculous happened: the union took Denise's case to arbitration and won and got her job back. And Amy was really impressed by that.

For Amy, residents' rights and her rights as a worker are deeply connected. Residents are dying because they aren't getting proper care. If they get a small sore on their butt and people aren't taking the time to wash it with soap and water, the wound grows and that is not good. *When we became CNAs we became advocates, and that's like taking an oath when you become a police officer or president of the United States. That's the way I see it. I took an oath that I would advocate for all my residents that I'm responsible for and I will. As long as I do this job, I will most definitely. It will be my life goal.*

For Amy, the American Dream means being treated equally like everyone else and having a good-paying job that pays a living wage and having enough savings to retire and enjoy what's left of life. She dreams of a time in the future where she can wake up and, if she's tired, she can choose not to go anywhere. That would be wonderful.

And she *does* believe that working-class people can still get there. But they have to work really hard. *I'm a firm believer in people having to work for a living. That's just how you make it in America, right? And lower-educated people have to work more than others. We have to work two, three jobs. But it's doable. It's hard work. But when it comes to the American Dream part, it's on the verge of that being over for the working-class people, unless you're holding down two, three jobs. But that means you sacrifice your family time, which causes a higher divorce rate. You sacrifice raising your children. So it's a vicious cycle. If they grow up alone, they get in trouble, they end up in prison. If they have kids, most likely their kids are gonna turn out the same because they're not given the same opportunity in a lower-educated family or lower-paid family, however you want to put that. But rich people, it's almost automatic, you know? The street has been paved for you. You don't have to really do anything, except go to college, which is wonderful. The opportunities are just unbelievable. You really can't help what family you're born into.*

That's what she tells her nephew Ryan: "You're not going to work in dietary all your life. You're gonna be somebody. But you have to work hard because you weren't raised in a family that has a great deal of money. So you have to work extra hard. But once you get there, you're gonna be so proud of yourself, cuz you did that yourself."

Ryan has a lot going against him: his working-class background, his autism, a speech impediment. It's hard to say he's got equal opportunity. But Amy certainly is doing her best to make sure he can find his way to the American Dream, even as it seems to be disappearing for folks like them.

Amy's dad was a firefighter who raised her after he and her mom got divorced. He ended up being the fire chief, and he's a big Trump guy. When he found out Amy was gay, he said, "Honey, are you happy?"

"I'm very happy, dad."

"Are you sure you just haven't met the right man yet?"

"Dad, that's the thing. It's not a man that I want to be with. I'm attracted to a certain female, which happens to be my partner. I'm not like those that you'll see on TV where they just go to a bar and sleep with anybody and everybody. That's not who I am, Dad. I've never been like that. I want to be with somebody that I can love and build a life with. That's Janet."

In the end, he just wanted her to be happy. Janet's mom, too, is very conservative—an evangelical Christian. But she, too, loves and supports her daughter and just wants her to be happy.

Trump ended up splitting Janet and Amy's household. Janet, a registered Democrat, voted for Trump because she liked that he wasn't a politician and thought he was good at building the American economy up because he's rich and not worried about bringing in funding like other politicians, whereas his treatment of women put Amy off too much, even though he did put money back in her pocket, now that she thinks of it. She couldn't get past his personality, but once he won the election, she accepted it immediately. *If it's best for our country, the American people will vote that way. And I'm okay with that. Once you're our president, you are our president. You have a lot of people like, well, Biden's not my president. No. Unfortunately Biden is. He truly is. And when Trump was our president, regardless of if I liked it or not, he was my president.*

Amy can't help but notice how much harder things have gotten under Biden. And she's not on board with a lot of what she hears from Democrats in Washington. For example, Amy doesn't believe children should be allowed to undergo gender transition. When she was younger and realized she was gay, her first thought was, *maybe I should have that surgery and then I could be straight—a straight man. And maybe my family would be okay with that.* She really thought about it that way. But as she grew up, she realized she didn't want to be a man. She wanted to be a *lesbian*—she *was* a lesbian. *I'm still a woman. And I'm really glad I didn't do that, I didn't have that opportunity to do that. Cuz I would've probably made that decision and then regretted it later on. I just want to be me, and people should accept that. For parents to allow kids so young to do it, I disagree with that.*

She also doesn't think children belong at drag shows. She went to one, and one was enough. *That is adult entertainment. It really is.* Her brother's brother-in-law and his husband are both drag queens for a living, and Amy bets *they* probably don't think it's appropriate for children.

But she also doesn't agree with holding establishments responsible. Put it back on parents. *Why don't you make a law that says if you take your kid to a trans show or whatever, we're gonna arrest you? How many kids will go then?* In general, she finds Florida governor Ron DeSantis's messaging around the issue alienating and exclusionary, even on the issues where she agrees with him. If Republicans portrayed themselves as the pro-family side, not the anti-gay side, that would probably go over a lot better. Because Amy, too, doesn't approve of the promiscuity she sees championed in some corners of the LGBT community.

Even on abortion, Amy's views are complex. She doesn't agree with just waking up and deciding to have an abortion. She doesn't agree with eighth-month abortions. Her sister had one just because the daddy didn't want another kid, and Amy did not approve of that. She sees a lot of younger people who use it as a kind of birth control, and that makes her uneasy.

But though Amy has things she doesn't agree with on the Democratic side, she always ends up voting for Democrats, for the simple reason that she can't get a meeting with most Republicans. Republicans are against the unions, and Amy truly doesn't understand why; if it weren't for her union, she'd still be making $10.40 an hour. She and her coworkers would never get to see their families, because they'd have to take on a third job just to make ends meet. *This work is really hard. Why is that a Democratic issue?*

She did get help from one Republican, once. Amy managed to get a meeting with a local Republican representative, and Amy asked her to help them change some laws to get some more job security. Amy said, "I want you to come down and see my facility," and this Republican actually came, and when she saw the facility, she said, "My God, this building is disgusting."

And Amy said, "Yeah, the building *is* disgusting."

When Amy started thirty-three years ago, it was pretty nice. But these days, the employees don't take much pride in their work. Anyway, Amy's union gave the Republican money for her campaign, and she won, and she actually did vote for the nursing homes when a vote came up. She voted for the workers. They were trying to increase the minimum number of hours a patient gets from a nurse or CNA. Right now, it's 2.9 hours in a twenty-four-hour period. *Doesn't seem like a lot, does it?*

But now it's even worse: It's only two hours. They dropped it again.

———

Gord Magill, the trucker who counts the stars though his windshield in the early hours of the morning, is originally from Toronto, though he's lived in Ithaca, New York, for years now. Forty-six, handsome, and lean with a permanent squint, a stylish flair, and a sonorous, gravelly voice, Gord—Gordo to his friends—has the benevolent raffishness of a pirate. He's been a truck driver his whole working life. The first thing he does when he gets in his truck is take off his boots. It's more comfortable—and it conserves the shoes.

His dad left right around when Gord hit puberty, leaving him with an unstable mother who drank, making him the man of the house at thirteen. He started working, getting jobs to help support the family, until he was working sixty hours a week while still in high school. He just barely graduated, what with all the lateness and getting lippy with the administrators giving him a hard time.

He got his first job in trucking at fifteen. There was a truck repair shop in town, and he'd bike over after school and on the weekends. He would grease trucks, clean up the shop, help the mechanics out, whatever he could. In the summers, he learned how to do things like replace the deck boards on the floors of trailers, which gave him a background in carpentry, too. From that he graduated to going with the guys down to the local mill and helping them tarp their loads and chain them down to the flatbed. As long as you could handle the ribbing and roll with the punches, giving back as well as you got, an essential part of working-class culture, you were one of the guys, one of the grownups, part of the group.

By the time he was eighteen, he was doing local runs around Toronto and southern Ontario, with the occasional mission to Montreal or Detroit. He then graduated to hauling steel loads down to Michigan, and when that got old, he went to New Zealand and hauled logs for a few years, before coming home and running up on the ice in the winters, hauling fertilizer in Saskatchewan seasonally.

In 2011, he met his wife Jenna, who remembers the first time she heard Gord's voice through a friend's phone even before she met him. Jenna and her friends were planning a trip to Burning Man, the hippie artist festival in the desert, where Gord was driving the ice truck in exchange for a free ticket. When the group arrived at Burning Man, there he was, and they just fell into it. Later he came to visit her in New York and they went to Occupy Wall Street together, and then Jenna went trucking with him in Alberta. When she hung off the side of the truck to pee in minus-thirty-degree temperatures, Gord knew he would never be on another first date again.

Jenna is a public-school teacher and a progressive, while Gord's views tend more to the right these days. Jenna was able to take some time off when she had their two girls. They were both born in the spring, so Jenna took the measly six weeks of maternity leave her job provided and that led into the summer break. They couldn't really afford for her to take off more time.

Gord makes $50,000 a year hauling logs for a local small business owner from clearing sites to a local mill. He gets up at 3:00 a.m. to drive out to the haul site, about an hour-and-a-half drive, pick up a load, and drop it at the mill. Then he'll go back and do a second haul. When he gets home around four, he's absolutely wiped, but that's his time with his girls. He's got to feed them dinner and get them to bed. Usually by nine o'clock, he's passed out.

Jenna also makes about $50,000. But even though they make more than the median household income in the U.S., they can't afford a home where they live, and they can't afford to move because Jenna's parents help out with childcare, which would be unaffordable in a place where home prices were more reasonable. So they, like so many other Americans, are caught in a Catch-22.

And they shouldn't *have* to move just to survive. *Some people really honor a sense of place where your family is, where you grew up,* Gord thinks. *That's an important component of some people's identity, and that's a good thing. When free-market types tell people to just move where the jobs are better, they are participating in the fracturing of American society. You make family formation more difficult. Your connection to your place is severed. And this is part of the reason why people are atomized and not going to church, because like our lives are being dictated by global capital and a lot of these* National Review *Cato Institute yahoos think that's just fine.*

There was a time in the not-so-distant past when trucking was a really lucrative job. In fact, it was exempted from overtime pay back in 1938 because truckers made so much money that the key was to keep them from working too many hours.

But in 1980, Jimmy Carter passed widespread legislation that deregulated the business side of trucking, which made it easier to get a license to operate as a carrier, opening up the market to more players but also putting a lot of the burden on drivers. These days, things are even worse. *They're trying very desperately to Uberize trucking, willing to throw any old mewling cabbage behind the wheel.* And to cover their backs, they have introduced a whole bunch of surveillance mechanisms in the cab to track how people drive. And then you need a whole HR department to track and rate the drivers.

This is where the libertarians have it right: you can solve a lot of problems by just not doing stupid things. On the other hand, the libertarian approach that resulted in shipping jobs overseas was obviously a huge mistake. They like to defend it by saying, hey, you get all this cheap stuff and the cost of living goes down because you can buy all this cool stuff. But the paradigm of moving those jobs overseas doesn't do anything for real estate prices here, which are only going up. It's not just about what you can put in your house. You have to be able to buy a house. And that is fast becoming impossible for me, which means it's gonna be more impossible for my kids.

Gord is not convinced that the American Dream still exists for folks like him. Hard work is no longer a guarantee of anything, much less a middle-class life. Until someone does something about the price of real estate, the American Dream will remain a fantasy.

———

There was an intersection in Flynn's hometown in Tennessee. On one corner was a Walgreens, and across from it was a vacant lot. As a little kid passing the intersection on the way to and from school, his mind would wander, imagining all the possibilities for the space. When he was six, he noticed signs of construction. They seemed to be building something big. And as they started to go vertical, he got excited, looking out every day to see what it was they were going to get. Then one day, when Flynn was six years old, the building was complete. Lo and behold, right across the street from that Walgreens, they had built a Rite Aid. It was the first time Flynn remembers feeling an emotion that would become his constant companion as he grew: he had to get out.

Luckily, he was good at soccer, and he got a soccer scholarship to a small college. He wouldn't have been able to afford to go to school otherwise; in fact, he sometimes sent money home from his work-study jobs to help out. He'd grown up lower middle class. His mom stayed home to raise them, and his dad, an army guy, worked a series of jobs before ending up doing real estate. There was no childhood home. By the time he graduated from high school, the family had moved houses more than twenty times. When there was money, they'd move somewhere nicer. When there was less, they'd move somewhere else. But Flynn didn't feel anything was lacking; even the people in town who had money were barely middle class.

He tore his meniscus at nineteen, but the school allowed him to stay on and switch over to a theater scholarship, and that's when he started acting; tall and slim with steel-cut cheekbones and a rakish forelock, Flynn found out he could also sing, and suddenly another career seemed possible. But he didn't finish college. He was bleeding money, even with the scholarship and his student loans. On a break from school, he auditioned for a job with Disney at one of their theme parks, and when he got the call saying he was hired, he grabbed it, thinking it would be the first of many. He was twenty years old, and the starting wage was $11 an hour.

He started out doing character work as a storm trooper, which required a two-week training period because there was a new technology created by Disney "imagineers" of the research and development arm of company that lets the storm troopers talk to guests with prerecorded phrases in the storm-trooper voice. Flynn loved using the new tech, seeing adults and children alike fascinated by it, and collaborating with other storm troopers about cool ways to use the stock set of answers in response to the questions people asked them. Sometimes the imagineers could come and ask them how the tech could be better, what phrases they found themselves wanting. The hours were long—there was one forty-eight-hour period where he clocked thirty-six hours at three different theme parks—but he loved working at Disney; you get to meet people from all over the world, and you really feel like you're part of something bigger, making magic.

He was offered a contract on one of Disney's cruise lines, which he accepted thinking there would be more opportunities for acting. It was an eight-month contract, and he would do meet and greets as male leads from Disney movies and under-study for the bigger roles. But by the end, he was ready to leave behind the tiny cabin and the sixty-hour workweek for which he was paid $600 a week. If he loved working at Disney, he loved working *for* Disney quite a bit less, a feeling that seemed to be common; almost no one renewed their contracts after the cruise ship ended. He didn't feel his input was valued, and there seemed to be a lot of magic left on the table, especially for male characters who were given less stage time. Of course, there were some people who had been doing the cruise line for ten years; one guy told Flynn, "This is my Broadway. This is all I really want to do."

But for Flynn, it was a stepping stone. In 2017, he and his wife moved to New York to take their acting seriously. It was rough: Flynn had to work three jobs to pay the rent. He worked at a rehearsal studio, he waited tables, and he worked retail. For a while he also worked at a museum devoted to *Friends* memorabilia. He lost a lot of weight; he's six feet tall and at some point, he weighed only 140 pounds. Then one day, he printed out twenty copies of his and his girlfriend's résumés and they picked a street in downtown Manhattan with some nice restaurants. They looked at the price points of the food and the clientele and scoped out the sections, trying to gauge how much money they would make. They both landed jobs at an upscale restaurant.

The job pays well: Flynn is making $1,700 a week, though he has no health insurance. It's a far cry from the Olive Garden he used to work at in a crummy corner of Orlando, where people would frequently walk out without paying. He and his wife live in Jersey City in a two-bedroom that costs them $2,600 a month, which leaves some money for vacations and Broadway shows.

He still goes out to auditions in his free time, but it can be a demoralizing process. Walk out onto Eighth Avenue and Thirty-Fifth Street and you'll see them—long lines of twenty- and thirty-somethings lining up at six in the morning in the hopes that they will be seen by a casting director. Whether it's December or June, they're lined up there, waiting for hours for a shot at a role. Flynn has gotten roles, but not the kind he's hoping to land one day.

For Flynn, acting is the only thing that shuts off his internal monologue, keeps the depression and feelings of insignificance at bay, the only thing that makes him feel like he's exactly where he's supposed to be. It's the only place he gets the peace that comes from feeling you are essential, important, bringing something only you can bring to the table. It's the only thing that makes him feel like he inherently matters.

That's his American Dream: to be able to act in something that has meaning for him, and that people will see. But so many people have the same dream, and he doesn't know if it's still a reality. So much of succeeding in any artistic field is just chance. And as he's getting older, he's getting tired of being tired. He's not sure how much longer he has it in him to do the starving-artist lifestyle. He wants to have kids, and he doesn't want them to struggle because of decisions he made in his twenties.

Could he be fulfilled in another career, something more stable and sure like teaching, or coaching soccer? He may have to find out if the acting thing doesn't happen for him.

━━━━

Linda isn't living the American Dream, but she thinks she's closing in on it, despite some major setbacks—a bunch of credit-card debt, a home she and her husband lost to foreclosure, the inflation that's got groceries so high. She lives in West Virginia. She's forty-six and she's been working for Amazon for almost four years as a driver out of an Amazon warehouse in Maryland. It's the best job she's ever had, and if she can stick it out, which she has every intention of doing, she'll soon be able to pay off her credit-card debt and buy a piece of land to put a double-wide on it. That would be her American Dream, and for the first time in a long while, it's in sight. She hopes to stay at Amazon for a long time. *I'm not planning on going nowhere.*

Before Amazon, Linda worked for an Ulta Beauty distribution center. She liked that job, too, but when COVID hit, they laid a lot of people off. No one was buying makeup without anywhere to go.

Now she works ten hours a day, four days a week. And she loves it so much she's jonesing to get back to work after the third day off. Her starting salary was $16.50 an hour, which is much higher than West Virginia's $8.75 minimum wage. And the benefits started right away.

A typical day starts at eleven. She signs into the app on her phone, which gives her her route for the day, and then she loads up the truck with big bags that are sorted so the first bag has her first fifteen stops in it, and the second has the next batch, and so on.

Linda was born in Oakland, Maryland. She grew up on a farm in Dickerson, where she was raised by her grandparents after her parents died when she was seven months old. She worked the farm as a little girl, riding the horses, milking the cows. *I've been working since I was old enough to talk. I can't not have a job.*

Linda went to school, too, and started high school, but she didn't graduate. She got pregnant at fifteen and left to raise her baby. Basically, she had to learn how to be an adult at that point—fast. *Nowadays I would tell kids not to even do it. Don't even think about it. Live your life first and then do it.* She's proud that her daughter has a career and no children—that she chose to establish herself at work first. Her daughter is a pig veterinarian, and Linda is extremely proud of her.

Back when she was fifteen and had to raise her daughter, she got a job working nights at a grocery store, then a gas station, while her daughter's father watched the baby. Then he would go to work during the day and she'd watch the baby.

Still, despite the difficulty of not having a high-school diploma and a struggle with dyslexia, at around twenty, Linda was overcome with the feeling that she could do anything she wanted to do. It was a palpable sense of opportunity and freedom. And what she wanted to do with that freedom was work.

She found her dyslexia didn't stop her from doing any kind of job she wanted. She's done manufacturing. She's worked at the humane society. She's worked at gas stations and for a book printer and an ink operator. She worked for the White Pages, making sure everyone's addresses were legit for the post office.

And of all those jobs, the best one she's ever had is Amazon.

Her boss worries about her and her colleagues more than he does anything else. He tries to make sure the workers are safe and satisfied, and to fix any problems that arise. If they need to take a break, he tells them to take a break. If they need the bathroom, stop and use the bathroom. Her boss tells her routinely, *I'm not worried about the vans, I'm not worried about nothing. Only thing I worry about is you and your safety.* It's like a gospel he preaches all the time. *The vans can be replaced, but my people can't.*

Linda thinks that in theory, unions are good, but she's been in a couple and has never felt like they did much to help her. She wouldn't want Amazon to unionize, because that just means more strikes to her, and less work. *We get paid good money to do what we do. Everybody's like, you don't make no money. Yeah, we do.* Linda gets a raise every ninety days. Now she's making $23 an hour, and she has full benefits.

She gets that some people have had bad experiences, but they make it sound like every job is bad, and that's just not been Linda's experience. *We don't get treated that way. It's just the people that's had a bad experience working for the company.*

Linda feels hopeful about her future, if only inflation wasn't so bad. *We're low-income people, and we live paycheck to paycheck. And sometimes we have to sacrifice one thing to do another.* There's been a lot of cutting back on what they buy at the grocery store since Biden took office. They try to buy and cook meals that will last a couple of days or more. Linda can't really think further than getting Biden out of office and replacing him with a new president. *It don't even have to be Donald Trump. It could be some other person that has more sense than Biden has.*

But of course, Linda liked Trump a lot. The economy was booming. Everyone she knew was living the good life. But not anymore. Linda can't afford to go on vacation this year. They usually go to North Carolina.

But Linda doesn't like the Republican Party, either. *They live the good life. They have money. But the low-class people doesn't. The low class works two or three jobs just to make ends meet.*

Both parties have abandoned the working class, Linda believes. And the rich get richer.

Linda's top priority when she votes is veterans—homeless veterans. It's just ridiculous how they treat them. She tries to help them out when she can, even slips them five dollars if she sees someone asking on the street. She's upset that so much money is being sent to Ukraine that could be spent helping veterans and also food banks.

And it upsets her that people who work hard but need a little help get nothing, while people who don't work at all or lie about their income get so much. That's what the Democrats represent to her.

What would help her most would be help with groceries. Food stamps for low-income people. No cash, just food only, just when times are tough. She doesn't believe in cash assistance. *Get another job.*

Linda knows a lot of people who are working very, very hard and still just cannot get by. She has a friend whose son is sick. The friend drives a school bus and has three children. One is in college, so she's trying to pay college tuition at West

Viriginia University for him to be a doctor, and her husband works full time too, and they still can't make ends meet. Linda has had to loan her money for food for the kids. Linda sent her son money in college to help them out. *It shouldn't be that way. Meanwhile, people who lie or don't want to get a job get all sorts of help from the government.*

West Virginia is the worst state for it. It's full of people who work extremely hard but still can't make it. There's a lot of people here, they have good jobs, they make good money, but for what they got, they can't afford it anymore. And to me, it's crazy. Some people make $50,000 a year but still need help paying their mortgage, their cable, their electric bill, their car. A car isn't a luxury. How are you gonna get to work without a car? They put so much on the system that only benefits the people who want to lose everything.

Under Trump, $200 would last a month. Now it lasts only two weeks. They can't get frozen foods anymore, frozen pizza, which used to be $5 and now is $9. It's $16 for hamburger meat. Linda is angry at the Biden administration for creating this economy and she's angry at the corporations for hiking up prices even further and stealing from hardworking people knowing they will pay it. And she's angry at the politicians who only think about the rich and never the working poor.

Politicians are always trying to buy her off with culture wars outrage, and she hates it. She doesn't care about any of that. *I don't care if you're purple, yellow, green. As long as you support yourself. It shouldn't matter what color or race or whatever you are. We all bleed the same color. My family was born in the South—that tells you how I was raised. But I'm not like that. My family was raised that "they" ain't no good. But to me, if they get out and make a living for themselves, they go out and do what they need to do, there ain't nothing wrong with that. They're just like me.*

Politicians are always talking about LGBT stuff. *That's nobody's business but the person who's going through it. Do you want to be with a man or you're a man and you want to be a woman, that's your agenda. I support you no matter what.*

Her ex-husband once asked her, "What would you do if our kids were gay?" and Linda said without missing a beat, "I'll support 'em."

Her aunt disowned her nephew for being gay, and he called Linda crying.

"Are you gonna disown me too?" he asked her.

"Disown you for what?"

"Didn't you hear that I was gay?"

"Yeah. So what's that got to do with me?"

Linda has two close friends who are gay. That's something that doesn't bother her. And she doesn't think that's about Democrat versus Republican. Personal issues are a person's personal business. *Why should we be a judge of that?*

There are houses falling apart in West Virginia that are empty, and there are people with no homes. Why don't they match them up with each other? Why don't our vets get any help? Why are people who work hard not given any help, but people who choose not to work get all the help they need? Why are the churches doing the government's job?

And she can point to specific Trump policies that brought down costs and put money in Americans' pockets. *He was bringing everything back over here. So people were making the money. Bringing back money from China. They can make it for $2, but to get it back here it's gonna cost a hundred. When you have an American company make it, we can make it and it will still be cheap.*

Linda's husband worked for a glassware manufacturer for decades—forty-five years in fact. Then in 2000, they shut it down and shipped it off to China and he lost his job. Linda began to work three jobs just to make ends meet, but it wasn't enough. They lost their house, a beautiful three-bedroom home on five acres. They fell behind on the mortgage—$900 a month that was just beyond their ability to pay. They had some savings, but their dog broke her leg, a little Chihuahua, and it needed to be amputated.

They took their $2,300 in savings and saved the dog and lost the house. Linda couldn't bear losing the dog; she already lost a daughter to congestive heart failure. *I've been handed the cards all my life.*

There should be some way, somehow that American people can be involved in this stuff. American people need to be able to go and have a conversation with our representatives and say, hey look, this is not working, and this is why it's not working. You're not thinking of the people, you're thinking of the money.

These days, it feels a lot like back in 2000, during the aftermath of her husband losing his job. And she thinks a lot of the epidemic of violence we're seeing—the crime wave across the nation—is the result of people being depressed because of the economy. Depression is a big thing in this country.

But though she isn't very hopeful about the direction the country is going in, Linda feels secure in her job and her own future. She's looking forward to owning that double-wide on a piece of land she's bought with the fruits of her labor. It shouldn't take her too much longer.

———

Jamie is a manager at a Home Depot in Vermont. He started out part-time and worked his way up to manager. The starting salary for managers is $60,000 a year, and the benefits are great, some of the best in the sector. He also has a 401K with Home Depot. All full-time employees have medical, dental, and vision insurance, and it's Blue Cross Blue Shield, so it's great insurance, and you can choose which tier you want so you can avoid high deductibles if you need to. Starting salary on the floor is around $16 or $17 an hour, and that's even for part-timers. It didn't take Jamie long to become a salaried manager, though. He had his sights on it from the beginning, and he made supervisor in a year and manager a year later. They called him the Rocket Man.

Jamie is from Colorado originally. His dad went out there because he was in the army, but he moved them back to Vermont because he got homesick. When Jamie was nineteen, he joined the Navy and served for four years. Being service oriented is a big deal in Jamie's family. They are proud of their heritage. His dad's ancestors were Dutch people who arrived in Manhattan in the early 1600s, and they have taken part in every major conflict in American history. Jamie does not take the idea of his civic duty lightly.

After he got out of the military, he did industrial construction on the East Coast, and then moved into residential construction, which he did for fifteen years. Things have a funny way of turning out, though. When he worked construction and he and his friends would go to Home Depot, he would tell them, "One day when I'm sick of being cold and smashing my fingers, I'm going to be a manager here." He now works at that exact same store as a manager. One day, he flipped some invisible, internal switch and decided to do something different.

Working at Home Depot is very different from construction. There's no PC culture in construction; it's very rough around the edges. It's a lot like the military. You have a job you need to accomplish and you just get the job done. Feelings come second to the mission. You've got to get the job done. Working at Home Depot is almost the opposite. It's very politically correct, which sometimes makes it hard for a guy like Jamie to just be quiet and play the PC game, seeing stuff you know is wrong but you're not allowed to talk about it.

And it's getting harder because of problems with the people he manages. The labor shortage has hit big-box stores hard, which has meant a lowering of standards. Stuff that would get you fired really quickly when Jamie was coming up is now tolerated. The corporate policy seems to be to let it slide. People will not show up for shifts, or they will be late, or they will have their earbuds in—a big no-no in a warehouse with forklifts and heavy equipment that can be super dangerous if you're not paying attention. But definitely the biggest problem is just getting people to show up to work and come on time. When Jamie gives his introduction speech to new hires, he tells every single one that if they show up on time, they will be a manager one day. And 99 percent of them can't do it. Over the course of two years, the company loses all but 10 percent of new employees, per Jamie's estimate.

Jamie is a philosophical sort of man. He develops theories about the world and then tests them out through the years through experiences. And his theory about why it's become so hard for people to hold down a job is that there is a crisis in the idea of the American Dream. For Jamie, the American Dream is the idea that the Founding Fathers had, that all citizens, no matter what race, color, or creed, all have an equal opportunity to that promise of life, liberty, and pursuit happiness. He thinks that idea is under threat due to pessimism and hopelessness he's seeing, which he believes is the result of the government creating too many safety nets. It's led to a crisis of confidence, vision, and purpose. A lot of people have no identity. They're lost—like the American Dream, which, if it's not dead, is dying. *It could be revived, but it's going to take a lot of hard decisions and sacrifice,* Jamie thinks.

This crisis in confidence has created a level of defeatism that's ironically coupled with entitlement for some. In Jamie's experience, a lot of people come to work at Home Depot with an attitude like, "This job is not my future," so they don't take it seriously. They have a negative way of looking at things, and don't take any pride in the work. They treat it like a joke, saying things like, "Well I just work here for now, I have a future career, and this is a joke." Jamie tries to tell them, "I hope you realize when you're my age one day, whatever your dream career is, you're gonna have people saying that about your dream career. It's just a job at the end of the day."

It's not like Home Depot is Jamie's dream job. He doesn't really believe in a dream job. Getting one is kind of like winning the lottery. Or they come and go. The military was a dream job; he absolutely loved what he was doing, and he believed in it, and a part of him regrets leaving, which he did for a relationship that didn't end up working out. But at the end of the day, a dream job isn't really realistic, Jamie thinks. If it was all fun, they wouldn't be paying you, would they?

Now he's focused on his wife and kid and having something he can count on during the next recession. In an uncertain economy, you could do worse than have a steady job with good benefits. Meanwhile his friends in construction keep telling him things are slowing down. So he's accomplishing what he wanted to accomplish. They were lucky enough to inherit a house; paying a mortgage payment would have been a struggle. Even so, Jamie doesn't feel financially secure by any means. What would make him feel a whole lot better is if the government showed American workers, American citizens, that we are the most important thing to them and that they are looking out for our best interests in their decision making. *Talk to us like we are intelligent people who can understand what they're talking about and get on board if we like it and not if we don't.*

Instead they hide the truth and they hide what they're doing, which makes people feel crazy, because the people in power want the doubt, they want the division. *At the end of the day, we all want the same things for the most part on a basic level: We all want to make a good living. We want to get our own house, we want to raise our families, however diverse they are. We want people to leave us alone about what we're interested in. There isn't even any real anti-gay sentiment left on the right. It's just left-wing agitprop that wants you to believe there is.*

Members of political parties pose as enemies to make Americans hate each other while consolidating around policy that enriches them and keeps them in power. And that divisiveness, it doesn't reflect the country—not at all. As a conservative living in Vermont, Jamie works pretty much exclusively with folks who are more liberal than him, yet they still agree on about 70 percent of the issues. One of those is how useless the political class is.

To Jamie, the pillars of a good life are like the coequal branches of government—you need them all: marriage, spiritual faith, and hard work. People think not working is freedom when the opposite is true. *I think it's very important for people to realize that your job does give you a sense of self. Your job does give you pride, your job gives you the freedom and the opportunities to do more. It's not the other way around. Sitting at home not working is providing nothing.*

———

But not everyone feels distressed at not being a homeowner. Courtney has worked at Starbucks since moving to Virginia from New Jersey two years ago. She's twenty-eight and lives with her boyfriend who works as a furniture inspector for a used furniture company. The company paid for the couple to move to Virginia, where they now rent a studio apartment together.

Courtney is Filipina, Puerto Rican, Irish, and Italian, but she considers herself white because the family spoke English at home. Her father built beds and then became a street sweeper before a knee injury left him on disability. Her mom is a waitress and a bartender and takes care of the family's elders. Courtney grew up with a lot of financial instability. *It wasn't to the point where we were gonna be in the streets, but it was hard for my parents to raise three kids. We were very close to New York, where it's really hard. You need a really good job to live in that kind of area, so it wasn't fully stable, but we got through it.*

Courtney wanted to become a chef, so after high school, she went to community college where she studied culinary arts. But she didn't pass some of her classes, so she decided to take a break from school, and got a job at the library before she and her boyfriend moved out to Virginia. That's when she got the job at Starbucks. At the time, she desperately needed a job and would have settled for anything, but it turns out Starbucks is a pretty good job. She really likes working there and feels the company creates a very positive atmosphere and pushes its workers to want to do better.

Courtney feels she's grown a lot working at Starbucks. She has a learning disability, and her memory is not the best, but her managers and coworkers have been patient and kind, and pushed her to push herself. *It's not that deep, it's just coffee, but they push me not to be scared, to make the drinks or whatever, and they have really good benefits. They pay for college courses, they pay for people that are trans and want to change—they pay for their surgeries. They're really pushing you to do better for your future and encourage you to succeed on things you want to succeed on. That's so nice. Overall, it's a great company.*

She usually works the closing shift. She likes to get to work early, which gives her time to have a coffee and relax, have something to eat, and talk to the regulars before she puts on her uniform. Then she'll step behind the bar and start making drinks. The most popular drink these days in the store is the ice brown sugar shake espresso. There aren't really any bad drinks on the menu, but sometimes customers will order something that really does not sound appetizing. Someone recently ordered a Frappuccino and ordered every single milk and syrup in that one drink. It was disgusting, maybe the most disgusting drink Courtney has ever had to make.

In general, Frappuccinos are the worst drink to make, because they have a lot of steps, and it takes so much time.

You have to get the pitcher and then get the cup, and put the milk in the cup, add the syrup they want, then dump it in the blender. Then there's the cream base and the coffee base, which is what gives it the Frappuccino texture. Then you add the top ends and the whipped cream. It's a lot. But Courtney loves being behind the bar, loves making hot drinks. It's fun and feels creative. Her manager encourages Courtney and her coworkers to experiment and try out new drinks on the customers to see if they like them.

The customers are great. Of course, you get a rude one every now and again, but for the most part, they are really nice and very encouraging. The regulars bring Courtney and her colleagues gifts, like the one couple who will periodically give them $10 gift cards, or cash at Christmas time, or the regular who brings them baked goods, or Steve, who orders them pizza. And when things get crazy behind the bar, the customers will call out encouragement to Courtney, like "Hey, you got this! You can do it! It's okay, take your time!"

Courtney feels like Starbucks cares about her and is invested in her success. When she fainted at work owing to the heat—the air conditioning was broken and they'd been waiting on the part to fix it for months—Starbucks paid for her visit to the hospital and for her to stay home from work while she recuperated. When she can't come in, her manager works hard to find a replacement. She feels like her manager really cares about the team.

Courtney is aware of the efforts to unionize some Starbucks locations, and her feelings on the subject are ambivalent. On the one hand, she thinks unions are great in theory. She knows they protect workers from being fired without cause, and that's really important. *I know they really protect workers.* On the other hand, she doesn't really see the point of trying to unionize her location. *I feel like I would push to become part of a union, but I don't see the point. 'Cause I'm not planning to work at Starbucks for the rest of my life, and I'm gonna say I'm okay for now. Like, we get raises every six months. So I don't mind not being in a union.*

Courtney can see herself growing with the company, taking advantage of its college program to finally take the courses to become a chef and pursue her dream. But she could also see herself becoming a manager at Starbucks. *Honestly, that would be amazing. I think very low of myself and I don't believe I could, but if I keep on working and keep on pushing myself, if I'm with the company for the next two, three years, I might try to become a manager.*

Courtney makes $16 an hour, which wouldn't be enough to cover her rent, which is $1,500 a month, but between her and her boyfriend, it's more than enough. She even has some savings. And they are able to spend time doing what they love—hiking, swimming, just generally being outdoors, and cooking together. Her boyfriend is Spanish and cooks really good Spanish food. Courtney's good at Italian, which she learned from her mom's side. She's been really happy in Virginia, which has felt like a fresh start for Courtney and her boyfriend. Their apartment is nicer than the one they had in Jersey. And she sees Starbucks as a stepping stone to pursuing a dream job, like becoming a chef, and her plan is to use Starbucks in that way. And for those purposes, it's a really great job.

She doesn't have plans to buy a home in the near future. She's very happy renting, and they might move to be closer to her boyfriend's son, who is in boarding school. And she can't say she feels totally financially stable; it gets a bit slow in the store in the summer, which makes it harder to get shifts. But generally she gets between thirty-five and thirty-nine hours a week, which qualifies her for Starbucks's health insurance. And she feels more stable than she did growing up. *I don't feel like I need to own a home. I'm okay with a decent apartment. I'm not like some people who need a big house, a big backyard. I'm very simple. As long as I'm living comfortably and don't feel like I'm suffocating in my home.* And she has that now. She has a view of the White House and a pool in her complex. There's a hot tub, and a pool table, and a gym. And she's able to save, too, which is a big deal.

For Courtney, the American Dream means living in a good place, working someplace good, having a bit left over so you can travel, and having the freedom to say what you want. She knows that's not true of all countries; anyone who's grown up with immigrants knows that. *There's a lot of good things about living in America and a lot of people moved here to pursue the American Dream, to get out of a bad situation from wherever they came from. And sometimes it feels like Americans don't realize how good they have it. A lot of them are like, America sucks, it sucks here, yada yada. But there's a lot of things I'm not afraid about in America. Don't get me wrong: there's some other countries that get free health care. Like there's a lot of things America can improve on, especially with the racism and all that. But I know I'm lucky. In some Spanish countries, you can't criticize the president, and we can say whatever we want about him. Some people don't consider what they have here.*

———

Some people still feel poor, despite being homeowners. Cyrus still feels like a poor kid in a forty-six-year-old body. Tall and rail thin with bleached blonde hair and fair skin and light eyes that more often than not are hidden behind sunglasses to protect them from the hot Arizona sun, Cyrus will forever feel poor because he feels he was deprived of the equal opportunity he is convinced a quality education would have granted him.

Cyrus works as a customer service rep for a Medicare Advantage plan. He makes $23 an hour taking calls from elderly people and directing them to the right office. It's a new career for him. For seventeen years, Cyrus drove a hazmat truck. He lives in Phoenix with his wife, Nona, who was also a trucker; for many years, the two worked side by side in the Haliburton oilfields.

Back in the day, the guys in management were blue collar, too, so they took care of the truckers. That's how Cyrus sees it. Or people were independent contractors who owned their own trucks. But all of that changed once you got this college-educated class in middle and upper management. *When a college-educated person sees me, they see white trash,* Cyrus thinks. *I'm subhuman, therefore, they're going to treat me in a subhuman manner. You're not gonna change that unless blue-collar people from a blue-collar background are able to go to college and become the CEO. Because right now, it's the college educated who set the rules of play we all have to live by.*

That class divide is the defining feature of American life. And to Cyrus, it's enraging. *If you're not full of rage, you're not working class. Because what it means to be working class in this country is to be exhausted.*

Cyrus and Nona are both artists. Cyrus makes art out of salvaged wood, gorgeous sculptures and woodworks that line the home he and Nona were able to buy through a government program after the two "divorced" so Nona could buy the home as a single head of household. This was after Cyrus and Nona spent a decade in the oilfields, working 100-hour weeks and making $14 an hour. Back in the day, trucking paid six figures. Guys would do it for five, ten years, build up a nest egg, then start a business somewhere. Today it doesn't pay nearly as much, and no one can afford to retire. Cyrus's coworker Jim is sixty-nine and still driving a truck. His body is spent. His eyes are shot, the veins in his legs are blown out from picking up heavy equipment, and he's got a rotator cuff injury in both shoulders.

Cyrus loved his coworkers like family. They got along in the way that blue-collar folks do, despite the political differences between them. Of all the truckers Cyrus has met, he'd estimate a third were Trump supporters, a third Bernie supporters, and a third of them were totally apolitical. Everyone is respectful of each other's opinions; not once in all his years trucking did he see a political fight break out.

Cyrus was born in Long Beach, California. His dad was a Vietnam War veteran who was exposed to Agent Orange and abandoned the family when Cyrus was young. Cyrus was bullied a lot. He had psoriasis, but there wasn't any money for the cream, and he had dandruff, but there wasn't any money for the shampoo. They ate out of cans. His shoes would break apart, the soles flapping loudly on linoleum floors at the local school, and the other kids would jeer at him. He tried to use Elmer's glue to fix his shoes and when it didn't work, he ripped off the flopping soles because the foam didn't make any noise. No one knows if your shoes don't have soles.

Cyrus started working as soon as he could, and his early twenties were a series of dead-end jobs making $12 an hour. He heard that his brother-in-law was making $20 an hour trucking, so Cyrus thought he'd try it too. He put the $2,500 to get his CDL on a Discover credit card (later written off when they got "divorced" and Nona declared bankruptcy) and started trucking, eventually ending up driving a hazmat truck.

When you're driving hazmat down a highway, you can't suddenly take your foot off the accelerator. There's no short stopping, or even quickly slowing down. In a few places in the country, it's legal to affix two loads together, a caravan of tankers, meaning you're essentially driving a 100-foot bomb. If you stop, you blow up. That means even if you find yourself driving behind a herd of deer, there's nowhere to drive but through, heads and legs breaking apart from bodies and flying into the snowbanks by the side of the road. Then you get to see the bones in the spring when you come back through. The first time it happened, it scared the living daylights out of Cyrus. The second time it happened, it became fodder for his art.

But Cyrus feels cheated out of who he was supposed to be. A nimble, analytical mind, a sharply observant nature, and a heart that rages for justice, he would have made a good lawyer. He desperately wanted to go to college, which he thought of as the way you get out of poverty, but he was too broke to afford it. He couldn't afford not to work, couldn't afford student housing, and couldn't afford the tuition.

There are a lot of Americans who aren't able to be who they were meant to be in this country, is how Cyrus sees it. He doesn't believe in the American Dream. It's for other people, not grown-up poor kids like him, and not his fellow blue-collar workers.

His most fervently held belief is that a good-quality secondary education should be free so that every American can decide for themselves who they want to be. It's deeply unfair that their tax-payer dollars are going to support institutions of higher learning where rich white kids get to self-actualize, and others get noth-ing. *You won't know the true potential of a nation until everybody is allowed to become who they are supposed to be. Americans like to be told that you as an individual are in control of your destiny. That's only true if we have shared resources that I'm gonna access and you're gonna access. They will benefit you because they benefit me and they will benefit me because they benefit you.*

Cyrus finally gave up on trucking. He did a program called Merit America that retrains workers. They taught him how to do tech support, how to write a résumé (*You put all these nonsense words together that literally mean nothing, it reads like gibberish, but then you get a call and a job*) and that's how he got the job with Medicare Advantage. His new job is also a new vantage point on American desperation. *American poverty is hardcore and it is entrenched.* He takes inbound calls from a lot of older people that are getting kicked out of their apartments because the rent's gone up and they have no place to go. *I worked with working-class people and now I'm working with old working-class people and I see it just gets worse. And it's getting worse—for everybody.*

CHAPTER 3

RISING

In the first two chapters, you met working-class Americans struggling to achieve the stability we associate with a middle-class life or the American Dream. And yet, they aren't the whole picture. There are plenty of pockets of American life where working-class Americans *are* living what they would call the American Dream. How do you quantify something like the American Dream? For many of the people I spoke to, it meant covering their bills with a little extra in case of emergencies. For others, it meant owning their own home and having enough to retire on. For others still, it was a more ephemeral, almost spiritual state of being at one with your circumstances.

Because the cost of living across the nation varies so much, income isn't the best way of measuring whether a person is middle class. After all, your income is a lot less important than what you can buy with that income. And whether you can buy a home is considered one of the most important factors of a middle-class life, according to working families.[1]

The good news is that many working-class Americans own their own homes. Police officers, firefighters, train operators, and pilots all have a homeownership rate well above 80 percent. Correctional officers have a homeownership rate of 84 percent. For firefighters, it's 81 percent. It's not just civil servants, either. For barbers, the homeownership rate is 63 percent. Manufacturing, too, still secures many Americans a middle-class life. The average homeownership rate of American workers in transportation and warehousing is 59 percent, five points higher than it is for service-industry workers. The skilled trades are another avenue that consistently pay a living wage. More than 70 percent of surveyors, draftsmen, electricians, cabinetmakers, plumbers, and pipefitters are homeowners.[2]

It's hard to get a quantitative feel for how many Americans are part of the working class that's living a middle-class life. In 2010, of Americans making between $20,000 and $80,000 year, 27 percent were making between $60,000 and $80,000 annually, with 13 percent making more than $70,000 a year. According to the American Community Survey, there are slightly more than one million police officers and detectives in the U.S., nearly 400,000 firefighters, 43,000 correctional officers, 135,000 barbers, and three million janitors and building cleaners. There are 700,000 electricians.[3]

Skyler Adleta is one of them, a twenty-nine-year-old electrician who lives with his wife Lauren and their two children in a beautiful, green Cincinnati suburb. Tall and broad with a jet-black beard and black-framed glasses, Skyler has the calm bearing that a certain kind of man takes on in the presence of women and children—the kind whose confidence comes from their ability to provide for their families with their hands. On the Memorial Day weekend that we met, he and Lauren had friends over, and their home was full of the joyous cries of children running in and out of the home while the grown-ups talked, periodically interrupted when their plotting went awry.

Skyler and Lauren went to school together, but it wasn't until in senior English class that Lauren started to notice the perplexing, smart yet irreverent boy who never seemed to have what he needed and asked her for a pen every single day. She didn't know that he was homeless.

One rainy day when she was driving out of the school parking lot, she saw Skyler walking through the downpour.

She pulled over and asked him if she could give him a ride; Skyler parked far from school because you had to pay for the school parking lot and he didn't have any money. It became their ritual: after class, Lauren would pick Skyler up in her car and they would talk about the books they were reading and their plans for the future as she drove him to his car. It was a while before she realized he was living in it, and then they talked about that, too.

At the time, Skyler's parents were divorced. His dad, an alcoholic, was in the midst of a legal battle over his eighth DUI and was living with Skyler's grandparents. He was about to serve a sentence, so Skyler couldn't live with him. And his mom had been cycling through a series of men, marrying them and getting divorced right after, which meant there was a constant shuffling of kooks through the house and a lot of uncertainty. Sometimes she was just gone for days on end. Skyler started staying at friends' houses when they'd let him, but one day when he tried to go home, his mom wouldn't let him back in. She told him he'd made his choice, and anyway, her apartment was in foreclosure. That's how he ended up sleeping in his car.

For their first official date, Lauren and Skyler decided to go hiking, because Skyler had no money. When he went to pick Lauren up, her father shook his hand for a long, long time, staring hard into Skyler's pupils and sizing him up. It was only later that Lauren realized that she'd basically said to her dad, "Here's this homeless boy—he's going to take your daughter into the woods!" But Lauren's parents were extremely gracious about the situation. They trusted Lauren, trusted her judgment—up until they were dropping her off at college four months later and she started to yell, "I don't want to be here! I'm just going to marry Skyler anyway!" That scared them—their seventeen-year-old daughter being that serious about a boy with no future and no prospects who lived in his car.

Lauren stayed at college, taking classes and working full-time to help Skyler pay for a place to live, but she eventually dropped out. They both worked at Trader Joe's, and then Skyler got a union apprenticeship as a plumber, but it didn't go well. Due to union regulations, he was expected to work at a much slower pace than his eighteen-year-old self, bursting with energy and ambition, could handle, and there was little room for questioning the rules—another thing that didn't sit well with him. Skyler lasted two weeks, and then left the apprenticeship and went to work at a local factory that made color pigment, where his dad had worked until his alcoholism made it impossible to hold down a job.

At the factory, Skyler made paint for everything from the siding on houses to the little black lines on the back of your car's rear windshield. He had to wear a respirator on the floor because of the metallic powdered pigment floating around in the air, toxic chemicals produced by firing and kilns the size of semitrailers that brought the temperature on the floor up to 120 degrees. The EPA required workers to shower at the end of every shift because of the chemicals, and as they stood in the communal shower, bright colors would wash off them and down the drain. When Skyler blew his nose, the tissue would be bright blue when he threw it away.

It was a terrible job, but if you could handle it, you got paid ridiculously well. The hours were 6:00 p.m. to 6:30 a.m. and two mandatory weekends a month, and there was unlimited overtime, plus hazard pay because of the chemicals. There were guys in the factory making over six figures. Skyler started at $17 an hour, and by the time he left five years later, he was making $28 an hour. It provided a solid foundation for the young couple, who got married during the paint-factory years and bought their first home. Lauren was able to finish taking classes and get her degree.

He would have stayed longer, but Skyler came up against the college glass ceiling when a management position opened up at the factory and his bosses, who he knew liked him, refused to even consider him for the position. So Skyler left to go back to the trades. He took a nonunion apprenticeship in electrical work where they taught him how to do the work on the job, and he went to night school. It wasn't even about the opportunity to make more money. Skyler had a sense he'd be good at leadership, and he wanted to work somewhere where once he earned it, he'd have opportunities to lead. He and Lauren talked to some friends and family who were in construction and decided that construction might be one of the last bastions of industry where experience is still the most valuable thing. Skyler was in search of a meritocratic industry where his skills would take him as far as he could go, where there weren't arbitrary gatekeeping requirements like a college degree for advancement in a field where practicality was premium.

He found it. The electrical apprenticeship was supposed to be four years, but two years in, Skyler was promoted to project manager. A few years later, he and Lauren were able to buy a new home in a beautiful, leafy suburb next to a country club with a big back yard for the children to play in.

Skyler is twenty-nine, a formerly homeless teenager who had managed to claw his way into the middle class in an ascent that is far from over.

But Skyler worries that the road he traveled is a narrow one, and he worries about the American working class. Young people are taught what he was taught, that to end up working class is to miss the train. High schools across the nation teach kids that if you don't get a college degree, you're doomed. They are taught that the only kids who go to the career center are losers.

This isn't just demoralizing for students for whom college isn't right. It's resulted in a vast deficit of people who know how to maintain our civic infrastructure. *We have a massive shortage of skilled trades in America right now*, Skyler thinks. *It's a huge problem* and it's tied to the fact that no one looks to the stars at night and thinks, "One day I'm gonna be an electrician." It's pragmatism that leads you to the skilled trades. You have something you have to do, take care of a family, take care of yourself. But this pragmatism can have huge benefits. It can yield huge opportunities. If you don't just do the bare minimum, if you stick around and hone your skills and your experience, you can rise up in a company, become somebody, keep applying and achieving and be whatever you want to be. You can run the company or start your own.

The problem is that there are all too often arbitrary barriers to climbing the ranks, things like having a college degree, which puts college grads in charge of workers who have no idea how to do those workers' jobs, have no idea what's possible and what's not. *Working-class people should have a shot at those jobs—they shouldn't be training people who know less than them to oversee their work just because that person got a college degree in some generalized field like "chemical engineering," who is completely inadequate to do the task that they're being expected to do, and doesn't understand the working-class culture they've entered, the intensity of the guys they've been put in charge of.*

The project managers for a lot of general contractors that Skyler's company is contracted out to are increasingly young college grads who don't know how to build a building, and they are unprepared for the viciousness of the men they are supposed to be managing. *That's the thing about the working class: If you're not one of their own, they will tear you apart, and they'll do the thing that in a corporate job, no one would ever do: They'll tell you "You're an idiot and I'm not gonna listen to you." So then these college kids end up hiding their ignorance behind being demanding and being a jerk—which all these guys see right through.*

This is not to say the American Dream is dead. Skyler wouldn't want to live anywhere else, wouldn't want to be working class anywhere else. He believes that if you're willing to put in work and investment, you can still hope for some level of exponential return in America. If you're competent, you're a good communicator, and you're willing to work hard, willing to be mentored, you can still achieve the American Dream. After all, he's the poster child for it: *ten years ago, I lived in a car, and now we have our home and Lauren gets to stay at home with the kids. But the blue-collar spirit that I remember seeing on, like, TV as a child—that's not there. A lot of them are pretty frustrated. They are making a decent enough living, but they have no advocates.*

And that bothers Skyler a lot. It shouldn't be that way. The trades are the frontier of America if you don't have a college degree. It's still a real meritocracy; you're going to rise based on your skill and talent. *Ability and competence will afford you a greater position, but personal responsibility and continually delivering on it will determine whether or not you keep it. As far as the employees that I see and deal with, if you do that, if you care, you show up on time and consistently work hard, you're in very good shape.*

But the *spirit* of the working class is crushed. The young people are crushed. And there is almost no one representing their voice in the American public sphere. And that makes people want to escape. It's the slow extinction of the working class through silencing and contempt. And that's very dangerous, because without the working class, there's nothing between poor and rich. You have a society made up of a few people with a lot of money and many more people with nothing, which isn't just unfair—it's destabilizing.

Yet no politicians that Skyler knows of are speaking to this issue at all; instead, the politicians who are supposed to be on their side seem to be totally invested in picking culture-war battles with other elites, and even if the working class agrees with them on those cultural battles, it seems self-serving and irrelevant to their actual needs. *I know extremely intelligent, competent people who are in the working class who find wokeness completely abhor-*

rent and unhelpful, but they also are, like, when is our leadership going to actually achieve some measurable thing for us? Everyone Skyler works with agrees with Republicans that children should not be exposed to sexually explicit materials in schools or have gender posed to them as a choice about their identity. But, there is also frustration that the issues that matter most to the elites in power are *all* they are willing to talk about. *It would be great if you could get transgenderism out of school but what's beyond that hill? What's on the horizon? No one's telling us, there's no promise at the other end, and that's frustrating. What are your meaningful legislation initiatives to bring back working-class life?*

Trump did talk about these issues, and Skyler voted for him, twice. But Trump was so maddening to the other side, so polarizing, that in the end, Skyler isn't sure it helped with the problem, which is the perception of the working class in twenty-first-century America. If the goal is to revolutionize how the working class is seen, it was counterproductive to have someone as hated as Trump representing their interests, even though he did it well from a policy point of view.

A leader who was one of them, an authentic representative of the working class with the pragmatism that defines it, would do a lot to help the morale in the working class. *People are so tired of feeling like dirt.*

The narrative that if you don't get a college degree, you missed the train needs to be changed. America needs to relearn respect for the working class—for the pragmatism that is there with the working class. If we actually want to heal the partisan divide in this country, all tribes have to be present. Because no one is going to be happy with something negotiated on their behalf—and poorly at that.

America needs a revival of the *romance* in working-class life, and for Skyler, that romance is caught up with his own personal narrative. Even as a homeless teenager, he felt he was called to a higher purpose, part and parcel of a life of faith that calls him to do whatever he does with as much integrity as he can muster, with the most servant-hearted spirit he is capable of. His faith enabled him to create a romance around his suffering, to imbue it with spiritual meaning so it didn't feel just hopeless. And meeting Lauren and getting married young lit a fire under him to become a provider, and a good one. Because she chose him and stuck with him when he wasn't a good bet.

If he had one message about the working class, it would be this: *These are human beings with very realistic expectations and desires from a social and economic standpoint, and we have to encourage the distribution of respect to them as well, not only for their own dignity but so we don't have industries collapse—and by extension, the country.*

You don't have to live in Ohio to be a working-class homeowner. Though New York boasts some of the highest home prices in the nation, 61 percent of service-industry workers are homeowners. If you ask Detective Patrick of the NYPD whether working-class people still have a shot at the American Dream, he will say yes, and he's found the formula. It can be summed up in two words: work hard.

Tall with high cheekbones, dark skin, warm dark eyes, and long, thin gray braids that he puts up in a big black knitted hat while working, Detective Patrick has an approachable aura and a quick, intelligent mind. He's always putting things together, finding patterns in what he sees, questioning orthodoxies, and trying to learn more about the world—and his role in it.

The expectation that you work hard was a big part of his upbringing. He was raised in the Bronx in the sixties by a Haitian mother and a stepfather. There was no talk of politics in the home; unlike many of his friends, Patrick's was not a Black Power household. Patrick's mother focused on making sure she went to work—she was a nurse's aide—and got the children fed, got them whatever they needed. His stepfather was abusive, and Patrick is still traumatized by it; he couldn't bring himself to go to his stepfather's funeral. Yet as he's gotten older, he's also gotten more torn about it. *He probably saved our lives*, he often thinks. While Patrick's friends were getting in trouble, first with their parents and then with the police, Patrick was too scared of the beating he would get at home if he joined them. His friends were a bunch of deviants, into guns and drugs and fighting, always running from the cops. Everywhere they went, there was a problem. But Patrick never got in trouble with the cops, and now he is a cop. And a part of him has to give credit to the man who traumatized him throughout his childhood, especially when he sees the names of his friends from the Bronx come up in the system.

His high school in the Bronx was pretty much all Black and Latino, and his first exposure to a mostly white population was when he went to Ithaca College. It was also where he first encountered critical race theory. *A lot of the things I'm hearing nowadays is what I heard back then*, he thinks. *It was the first time I heard this idea that Black people can't be racist because you don't have power.* Of course, he bought it back then. It bonded the few Black and Latino students at Ithaca College and Cornell. Back then, Patrick wanted to become a filmmaker, wanted to tell stories of Black empowerment, about stereotypes Black people struggle with, what it means to be a Black man in America. It was right after Howard Beach, and Tawana Brawley, and Bernard Goetz. *Now when I hear stories like that, I research them*, he thinks. *Back then, I just accepted it, and it shaped my mentality.*

He graduated from Ithaca College in the 1990s and moved back to Crown Heights at the height of the crime wave, which meant he learned a lot about crime—as a victim, like everyone else he knew. He got a few jobs in the film industry, but he wasn't making any money and had to move in with his sister, who just didn't understand why a college grad couldn't get a job that paid. He lasted one year, and then abandoned filmmaking to cut hair. He'd made friends with a barber in the South Bronx who taught him well, and he made some good money. Then he got a job at the library, a salaried position, during which time he met the woman who would become his wife.

But the library wasn't where he was meant to be. Patrick had always fantasized about being a cop. He thought it would be exciting to be speeding down the street with the sirens on. (He was right; it is exciting, and it still thrills him twenty years into the job.) But it took him a long time to admit he wanted to be a cop, even to himself. *What they don't tell you is that being a cop in the Black community, it doesn't look right.* So he denied the attraction, denied it and denied it. His mom especially didn't want him to be a police officer, but after she passed in 1990, when he was thirty-one, he finally felt free to follow that calling and join the NYPD. He had a daughter, then a son, and by 2006, he'd made detective.

He now lives on Long Island, where he owns his home. His daughter is in college. He is planning to retire soon to focus full-time on his art—enormous, gorgeous oil paintings stacked by the hundreds in his basement. It is by all accounts the American Dream par excellence.

What he worries about is how little effort is being put into making it a viable pathway for the next generation. Despite being a major vector of economic stability, police officers, like other working-class Americans, have become the object of contempt, derision, even hatred in the mainstream culture. And it bothers Patrick—a lot—especially because it seems tied to a larger problem of crime plaguing poor Black neighborhoods, which keeps too many Black children in intergenerational poverty.

Patrick's greatest struggle is a deep-seated loneliness and inner turmoil that comes from the disconnect between how he sees himself and his work, and how he feels he is perceived in his community. He used to believe that Black people in America were something like the chosen people—unique and treasured because of the past of slavery and discrimination. *We've accomplished a lot. We've been through a lot, and we've gotten far in our whole experience.* Yet lately, he's been feeling differently, like the problems he sees on the job are largely self-inflicted, that the narrative spun by Black Lives Matter and other activists is largely an effort to cope with the truth without acknowledging it. While millions were out on the streets protesting police brutality in 2014 and 2020, Patrick was in his car, sirens blaring, following the orders of dispatch: "Shots fired."

How could that be? He wonders. *Here we are telling the world, look how we're being treated by the police because of our color—meanwhile, you have shootings in our neighborhoods, so many you can't even keep track of them. Whenever we're doing something on behalf of something wrong that was done to us, not too far away, someone else in our community is doing something too, undermining the exact point that's trying to be made. It's embarrassing,* Patrick thinks. *Here we are talking about all these things we're going through, that's happening to us, but then right down the street you have young kids getting shot. How is anyone supposed to take our plight seriously?*

I can't possibly be the only one who thinks this, he says to himself while driving back and forth to Queens from Long Island, while painting scenes of cops and Black people and the tragedies that play out between them. *But why am I not hearing this from other people more often?*

It's different than when he was young. Back then, kids would rob the kids who had stuff they didn't have. But these days, it's not about poverty. *It's about a power trip. To run up on someone and make them just give up everything—that's an incredible power.*

"Take off the gold chain bracelets. Take off your shoes," *whatever they want*. The explanations that people used for a lot of things in the past don't apply anymore. *We still think guys are doing these things because they're deprived. But some guys do this because they like the idea of you submitting to them. It feels like the robberies are done for sport.* It's almost a rite of passage these days. And it's just not about poverty. You have guys driving BMWs jumping out and robbing people.

The juxtaposition pains him, especially since the George Floyd incident. *You had all this activism and awareness being brought to the plight of the Black community. Everyone was contributing, you had all these commercials and things. Meanwhile, us in the police department, here's my sergeant, he comes along, he says, "Okay, here you got this case, gunpoint robbery, or this guy, he choked his girlfriend." So that means now I gotta go right back into the Black community. I gotta go right back into another situation again. We have to lock up another Black man for another offense. In the midst of all the George Floyd things going on, they are laying the groundwork for another potentially violent or deadly confrontation. 'Cause I have to take you into custody. And if we the cops are such a problem, then why do people keep calling us?*

They don't want brutal policing, of course. But they want policing. They want good policing. The problem is, the more crime there is, the more policing there's going to be, which means more opportunities for the police encounter to go bad. *We know it every time we go out and we're going to a situation, we know there's a potential for something to go bad. You do everything in your power and pray that it doesn't, but sometimes it just doesn't work and then it looks bad.* He tells it to guys in the street: *You never win battles with the police in the street, because in order for the cops to overcome your resistance, more cops are just gonna show up.*

At the end of the day, the police can't really stop the violence, Patrick thinks. Criminals aren't even afraid of the police anymore.

He's seen people shoot each other in broad daylight, right in front of police officers. Only the perpetrators can stop it. *It's gonna stop when we decide we want to stop.*

The thing about these guys he encounters, the criminals he arrests day in and day out, is they have another side to them. They can be like the devil, especially when they are engaged in the kind of behaviors that get them face-to-face with Patrick. But then he'll spend the night with a criminal, in the hospital, say, and he'll see another side. There are lovable elements to them, the part of them that appeals to their mothers, to their friends. Many of them have been sexually abused. Then they have this other thing that they do that brings the police into their lives, that brings out the worst in them and in the community.

Why do they do what they do? And why did I not do it, not go down that path? Patrick has been asking himself that question his entire life. So many of the guys he grew up with ended up like the guys he arrests. Every once in a while, he checks in on them, looks up their names in the system to see what they're up to, what they've been locked up for, what they're getting in trouble for, and marvels at the fact that they are in prison, while he is living the American Dream.

Of course, racism still exists. When he was in narcotics, a cop on his team, a white guy, used to hang a little plastic gnome from the ceiling that he referred to as "the wizard," as in the KKK. But most of the other cops on the team were Black, and they just needled him back. Nobody let it affect them that much. Today it would be a huge story, but it never bothered Patrick. The guy was a good cop. He always had Patrick's back on the street.

The hypersensitivity of today hasn't made him safer. The opposite, it's made his job a hell of a lot more dangerous, thanks in large part to the Black Lives Matter movement. It's put a strain on the police, made them second-guess everything, worry about how people are going to spin it. It's had a deep psychological effect on cops, which in turn has had a deep psychological effect on criminals, because when they see the cops hesitating, they see that as a green light. And of course, there's all the judgment in the media. Sometimes he looks at the way cops are talked about in the media and on social media and he thinks, *Does my wife see me that way? Does my daughter?*

What he needs is a society that respects the work he does. Because everything else he's managed to accomplish on his own.

———

It's not just cops and electricians and ex-military folks who have a good shot at being middle class. Even some people working in the service sector have managed to eke out the American Dream. According to the American Community Survey, as of 2021, the homeownership rate for janitors and building cleaners was 60 percent. For maids and house cleaners, it was 51 percent.

Elena is one of them. Petite and contained with curly hair that's still black and almond-shaped eyes that twinkle with a wicked sense of humor, Elena works as a guest-room attendant (or housekeeper) in the Mandalay Bay hotel and casino on the Las Vegas strip. She's had that job for twenty years, which was just three years after she came here from the Philippines.

Elena grew up in a province in the Philippines, where her father is a bus driver. She's been in Las Vegas for twenty-three years, twenty of them at the Mandalay Bay Resort and Casino. She makes $21.94 an hour.

She arrives at work at 8:30 in the morning and clocks into the floor she is assigned to. Then she gets a key to the floor and heads over to the pre-shift, where the floor manager explains what's going on, how many guests there are, what percentage occupancy the hotel is at. Then she gets the rooms she has been assigned and she goes to her station to load the cart and checks in again with the app on her phone, which lets her know if the guests have checked out of the room. Then she heads in and starts cleaning.

You meet people from all over the country, all over the world, as a guest-room attendant; people from the U.S. stay an average of five days, so she gets to know them. People from other countries stay longer, many for up to two weeks. The guests are all very kind, but the best guests are the ones who understand how she feels, let her do her job, and tell her they appreciate her work: people who acknowledge that housekeepers work really hard. Some guests tip, and some tip every day—that's really nice. Of course, some people leave just a few coins, but if you're lucky, you'll get ten bucks. Five dollars a night is a nice tip.

It used to be they mostly got convention people at the hotel. Convention people are easy to clean up after, because they're in and out. They come for a couple of days, they spend most of the time at their conference or expo, and then they leave. They aren't very dirty, and it's usually just the one person. But these days, they've been getting a lot of families at the hotel. Families are much dirtier. They spend a lot more time in the hotel room, and they generate a lot more dust and garbage.

Making matters worse, since COVID, hotels have done away with daily cleaning. Before the pandemic, Elena and her coworkers would clean the rooms every day, whether they were occupied or the guests had checked out. They would alternate one occupied room with one checkout, which meant you got an easy room in between every hard room. There's only so much damage a guest can do in twenty-four hours, so it kept the work in those rooms to a minimum, or at least a predictable amount of cleaning. But now, you get families coming to the hotel and staying four, five days, and no one has cleaned the room in all that time. Imagine what that room looks like when a guest-room attendant shows up after checkout: three, four days of trash, the Vegas dust coating everything, soap scum built up in the shower from the hard water, and the floor is always filthy. It takes at least twice as long to clean, vacuum, and sanitize a checkout as an occupied room. Now imagine having to do eight of those in a row, every single day. *Our bodies will be so tired. And we would get so stressed. And when you get stressed, that affects your health.*

The hardest rooms to clean are party rooms. As soon as you walk in, you know you've got a party room because of the mess—the balloons, the streamers, the soap bomb in the tub, the glitter, everywhere. When you get a party room, you report it: this is a trashed room. If a checkout takes about forty-five minutes to clean, a trashed room takes two hours. You have to report it so you get more time and don't get behind in your rooms and get written up. Then the floor manager comes and takes a picture of the trashed room, and you get rooms knocked off your list. Then they charge the guests for the damages.

Elena is worried that if they don't bring back daily room cleaning, there will be massive layoffs. She has a lot of seniority thanks to her twenty years, and she sees herself as responsible for her coworkers, especially those coming up behind her. It's one of the big things she's fighting for and fighting hard for in the current ongoing contract negotiations with the casinos.

Elena is an executive board member of her union, the Culinary Workers Union Local 226. She's been in the union for as long as she's been at Mandalay Bay. In fact, as soon as she was hired, the person who hired her at the casino gave her some paperwork and told her to go to the union. And she said, "Okay, sounds good." So she went to the Culinary Workers Union, and they explained to her that if she works at least four days a week, which she would be—the casinos are always, always looking for guest-room attendants—then she would get good benefits. She asked what the benefits were, and they told her there was health insurance—that's the most important—and a pension, which is also very important, because when you get old, you can look forward to some money. The union also guaranteed job security—at least forty hours a week, and respect for seniority that isn't disrupted even if the building is sold, which it has been.

In the ensuing twenty years, she was able to regularly send money back to the Philippines to family who didn't have the opportunities she did. The health care was better than she could have imagined; no co-pays, no deductible, no hidden fees. Just 100 percent covered. And she was able to buy her own home, which she owns with her husband. Today, the casinos chip in $20,000 toward a down payment for any union member—something Elena helped fight for that didn't exist when she bought her home, and she's thrilled every time one of her coworkers takes advantage of the program.

That's the American Dream right there: *to work here in Vegas and to have our home, our job security, to have good benefits, good pay, a good contract, and a good union. That's the American Dream. When you have the union, everyone is united. Everybody comes together to fight for a good contract. Imagine seeing all the housekeepers getting together to fight for a living wage, where one job is enough and you don't have to work a second job, and you can support your family, too.*

The union also gave Elena something more ephemeral than wages and benefits: a sense of pride and ownership in her work, a feeling of control over her destiny, a dignity in her labor. It gave her the security to enjoy her job, which she wouldn't trade in or even trade up. Elena was once asked by the casino if she wanted to become a floor manager. "No, thank you," she replied. They asked her why not? And she said, "If the floor manager is in the union, yes, you bet I will move. But no thank you."

Without the union, they can just fire you anytime they want. There's no security, no protection, and no overtime. Elena has four coworkers who were fired, but the union intervened and got them right back in their jobs. *That's how powerful our union is.*

And that power is irreplaceable. It means that Elena doesn't have to worry about whether her bosses appreciate her work or not, because she is fairly compensated for her labor. One day, her floor manager came around with a basket full of candies, the kind you buy in bulk from the dollar store and asked if she wanted some. Elena asked what it was for.

"It's appreciation day for the workers," he said.

"Are you kidding?" Elena replied. "The company makes billions of dollars and you're gonna give us this candy? And it's not even a Tootsie Roll? No, I'm good."

And she was.

———

Rory also lives in Las Vegas. He's from Northern California, about twenty miles north of San Francisco. He moved to Vegas in 2015 with his girlfriend, who's now his wife. Prior to Vegas, the couple had been traveling and working seasonal jobs in national parks and other resort towns—five summers in Montana, a couple of seasons in Colorado working in the desert resorts. Rory would usually get a job as a bellman—that was the job you really wanted, because of the tips. You had to know someone to get a bellman job. But there was always talk about how the really good jobs in hospitality were in Vegas; the benefits were good and there was a lot of stability because they were good union jobs. A few months after moving to Las Vegas, Rory got a job at the Flamingo, and he's been there ever since.

He was initially hired as a baggage handler, but he became a bellman after four months, and now he's working the graveyard shift. When he gets to work, he swipes his ID and gets into the digital queue—there's a whole separate technology for the bellmen—and when your name comes up, you swipe and get your ticket and go to one of the 3,500 rooms in the hotel that has asked for help. The hotel is so big that Rory walks up to six or seven miles in a single shift.

Rory enjoys his job a lot and thinks there's a definite possibility that he'll never work another job. There are people he works with who have been at the job for more than twenty-five years. There are inside bellmen and outside bellmen and valets, doormen, and someone running the taxi line. Everyone works together and helps everyone out, and in between, they talk about everything from family, to work, to politics; there's a real diversity of opinions. Las Vegas is no bubble; there are people who are happier with the current president and people who were happier with the former president and everything in between, but politics isn't very important to people. They're focused on their job, their family, their home, and their community. It's Vegas first, and America second.

Rory officially makes about $15 an hour, plus about $5 an hour in benefits. But it gets to be much higher with tips. He can make up to $200 a shift on a good night when it's busy and people are tipping generously, though there's a lot of variation depending on the time of year. It's enough for Rory to have bought a house in 2019, cover his bills, and save every month, even though he's now the only breadwinner; his wife is currently in graduate school getting a master's degree in creative writing.

At thirty-nine, Rory has already gotten farther than his parents, who never owned their home, and even the kids he knew growing up who were more affluent than he was can't afford to buy a home if they stayed in California, even the ones who got advanced degrees. But in Las Vegas that's normal, to have people working in the hospitality industry who are homeowners and planning their lives and their pensions. There's a high degree of financial literacy in this town, and it's all thanks to the union.

Rory makes $10,000 a year more than nonunionized bellmen, and the union ensures he has a regular schedule, which is rare in hospitality. He is pretty much always guaranteed forty hours a week in a way he can build his life around. There's a work/life balance in the hospitality industry in Vegas that doesn't exist anywhere else, and Rory and his wife spend a lot of time in the mountains, hiking, camping, traveling for one- or two-night getaways. The Culinary Worker's Union also helped him with the down payment on his house, makes sure he's able to save for retirement, gives him health-care coverage with no co-pays and no deductible for himself and his whole family, and he has a pension plan. And they are currently in contract negotiations with the casinos for raises. They are asking for $3 more an hour, which means that there will be at least a $2-an-hour raise when the negotiations are over.

Rory is a shop steward, which means he represents the union at his workplace. He talks to the younger workers who are just starting families, trying to figure out all the rules. The union is very pro-family, and the stability it provides makes having a family not just feasible but something people can prioritize. For many of Rory's coworkers, family is everything—it's the focus and the goal and the object of their search for stability. Stable families are a hugely important thing in Vegas. And people have them.

People don't leave these jobs for a reason. If the rest of the country is struggling when it comes to working-class Americans searching out the American Dream, it is alive and well for hospitality workers in Vegas. Vegas is about the dignity of working people more than anything else.

———

Eric grew up extremely poor in Pittsburgh. His father was a career job-loser; he was an extremely hard worker when he wasn't drunk. He worked in manufacturing when he could get out of bed, and it was tough making ends meet. They lived in a house Eric's parents got from HUD that was in bad shape. Still, his mother always found ways to make sure he felt like he had something, even though they didn't have anything. Eric never felt poor, probably because there was no one around him growing up any other way. No one ever took vacations, they didn't go to the suburbs, they didn't even really leave the neighborhood. *Everyone around me was poor so you didn't know no better.*

Kids in the neighborhood did a lot of drugs and a lot of drinking. By eighth grade, Eric was high at school more often than he wasn't. By the time he was twenty-one, he'd lost five friends to drunk-driving accidents or drug overdoses. He realized he had a decision to make: He could become his father, or he could choose something else. He chose something else. *Every day I woke up and said, "That is not the guy I want to be." I hated him as a teenager, because he wasn't there to guide me. I made the decision to stop everything, and I had friends who were willing to accept that. They didn't exclude me or shun me. They didn't make fun of me. But I stopped everything in ninth grade and said, "I am not ruining my life."*

It's not exactly true that Eric's father taught him nothing; he taught Eric what *not* to be. As far as what to be was concerned, Eric looked to his friends' fathers. And his friends' fathers had union jobs. Anyone in Pittsburgh whose family life was stable had a father in a trade union. So Eric grew up thinking that unions were the way out of poverty—period. And he still believes that.

Back then, about twenty-five years ago, Eric's high school was very oriented toward the trades. He went to a Pittsburgh public school where they had carpentry classes, basic electrical classes, and power-energy classes. In his senior year, the carpentry teacher took the students to take the union test for carpenters. She rented a van and took the whole class.

But Eric didn't want to be a carpenter. He wanted to be an electrician. There had been an elevator company across the street from where his mother worked when he was little, and the idea stuck with him: an elevator electrician—a *union* elevator electrician. That's the thing to be. But getting into the electricians' union was harder than he expected. He applied to the electricians' union, the millwrights' union, and the tin knockers' union right out of high school, but he was turned away three years in a row. Back then, there was a lot of nepotism, and he didn't have enough connections to land a spot. But every year after the interview, Eric would tell the interviewer, "If you don't let me in this year, I'll just see you next year. I'll be back." In the meantime, he worked constructions jobs to pay the bills and get experience, things he could put on his résumé. He would take jobs at electrical companies or construction companies that would hire him as a laborer and give him an opportunity to learn something.

After three years, he landed a job with an elevator company, which offered him a shop job as a welder's helper at $9 an hour. He was twenty-one years old, and he took it thinking he'd get his foot in the door, make a name for himself, get experience, and push his way up the ladder by showing his work ethic. It paid off. After three years, he ran the division and was making $21 an hour building the elevators that go up big television towers. And finally, three years after that, he got into the elevator's union. *It took six years—imagine waiting six years for a job. Sometimes it's tough to stick it out.*

Today, Eric would call himself middle class. He makes $140,000 a year and lives below his means with his fiancée and her son.

I'm not book smart. I can barely read when it comes to compre-hension. I'm extremely hands-on. There are people just like me that fail at high school, fail in classes, fail taking tests, but when you put 'em in front of something mechanical, they'll shine. They don't think the way other people think.

Eric is politically an independent, though he leans more conservative. But these days, he feels like neither political party in America represents workers. He sees a huge disconnect between union leadership and card-carrying members. The workers he knows, the guys on the job sites and the guys you see putting up buildings—they are extremely conservative. But the bosses and union management and companies are all extremely liberal. *But you just don't talk about it at work. You only talk about it with guys who share your views. My boss is extremely Democrat and I don't talk politics at work. I put that aside because I don't care, as long as he's writing my paycheck, I couldn't care less what his politics are. That's how we view it in the trades: You just don't talk about it.*

That's why he doesn't buy the idea that the reason people aren't joining unions is because the leadership is Democratic. He thinks it's more personal than that. Fathers aren't teaching their sons the power of unions. In many families, there isn't a father to teach them anything at all.

But it's not just the fatherlessness. The benefits of the union are long-term, and this is a short-term society. *Everybody in today's society wants instant gratification. When they sign up for a job, they want it right away. I waited six years on a list to get in my union. I waited it out. And some of these guys stick it out for just as long as I do if not longer waiting for this job to come about. But as soon as they get in, the first thing they do is worry about, "When's my raise? When's my raise? When's my raise? When's my raise?" They forget that they have to put the time in to get to that journeyman rate. I think a lot of people don't want to put that time. They won't sacrifice two dollars an hour today for thirty dollars an hour more in five years. They need that instant money. Unions are long-term money.*

Unions are not just money: He has great health care, with just a $300 deductible. He has great annuities. And he has a great retirement pension plan. *But all that comes with time. It isn't instant. To make it, you need someone to guide you, someone in your ear saying, "You don't want that, you want this." But you need to want it yourself, too. It's got to come from both places, for when you want to give up. You don't have to be extremely rich to live a decent life. You just have to work hard at it.*

———

But some people's struggle to achieve the American Dream is less financial, and more psychological—even spiritual. Benjamin West grew up middle class in Seattle until his parents, both schoolteachers, got divorced, and his mother took him to live in Arizona. Things went downhill from there. His mother got a job as a substitute teacher, but she only made enough for a small one-bedroom apartment, and they relied a lot on help from friends, local churches, and government assistance to get by. Ben went to a military program for six months, and then got an academic scholarship with a free ride to go to college. But it was 2003, and he could still taste the ashes of September 11. *I felt an obligation as a citizen. I had been given a free ride, like, "Hey, you got the scholarship," and I had a career-path plan, but with what was going on in the nation at that time, I felt this responsibility as a citizen that I need to go and fight the war, and if I don't do this, then I'm probably going to regret it for the rest of my life.*

Ben enlisted, and he deployed to Iraq four times—in 2004, 2005, 2006, and 2008. Then he deployed to Afghanistan in 2012. *My first two deployments, I still had Kool-Aid from basic training and media propaganda. It felt like I was in a holy war, some type of crusade, and I was fighting for the American people and the American way of life. But after my third deployment, I started to question things and think for myself a little bit and look at some data. And it started to become pretty disturbing when I looked at military contracts that were being given out, the government officials affiliated with those military contracts. And in the last four or five years, I started noticing the pharmaceutical contracts with Afghanistan, and then how that related to the opiate epidemic in the U.S. and veteran suicide and how many drugs they're putting vets on.*

Ben would get firsthand experience with all of it when he returned Stateside. He had three friends who were killed in combat overseas, but twelve of his friends have committed suicide since they got home. *The fact that we've lost more people Stateside due to depression and suicide versus actual combat—I think there's something there.* Ben himself suffered from post-traumatic stress and severe depression. When he got home, he didn't know how to process the loss, the rage, the hate leftover from spending months and months facing down people who wanted him and his friends dead. There was never a healthy transition back to civilian life, or back to active duty when he returned, which often involved special ops that went on for twenty-four to thirty-six hours; the medic would prescribe Ben and his friends Ambien the day before an operation so they would sleep through the day in preparation.

In 2007, he was blown up and medevaced, and he was given fentanyl while they were removing shrapnel from his lower extremities. He remembers not feeling a thing. When his best friend got addicted to fentanyl, Ben had a reference point. Like too many Americans, Ben's best friend—a solidly middle-class man with a family and good finances—started with opioids and before he knew it, he was addicted to fentanyl. *When he explained to me everything that happened, it really hit close to home. Young American men are struggling with this. It's an actual epidemic. I have a lot of empathy toward them because there has been an attack on masculinity—and recently an attack on femininity. And that's very discouraging, to both sexes, when one is demonized by the other side. I think it's taken a tremendous toll on the psyche of American youth.* Ben's friend went to a rehabilitation facility in Arizona and miraculously recovered. But Ben continued to struggle.

In 2020, he met a waitress at a sushi joint he often patronized in Georgia, and a friend pushed him to ask her out. He asked her if she wanted to get coffee and she very politely turned him down once, then twice, and then finally she said yes. They got married, but Ben wasn't able to be fully present. His wife had two children from a previous marriage, and then they had a child together, but mentally, he was somewhere else. His kids would ask him to go play outside, and he would say no. He just wanted to sit on the couch and do nothing. It was really tough on his wife and children. He couldn't feel the emotions he was supposed to feel. When his wife got pregnant, there was just a blank hole where the joy was supposed to be.

One night, he found himself staring down the barrel of a gun. *I came to a point in time where I was very disconnected and disassociated from my family, and I thought that the right thing for me to do to benefit them was to kill myself. And one night, I drank a bottle of booze and was staring at a firearm. And a friend called me up out of nowhere at two in the morning and just said, "Hey, man, how you doing?" And I was like, "Well, you know, I'm not doing so hot." And he was like, "All right, well, I'm gonna fly down there tomorrow and we're gonna hang out." Him and another friend kind of had an intervention. They told me, "You know, you gotta go somewhere and get help, man."*

Ben listened. His first attempt to get help was at an army hospital where the counselors were civilians who didn't understand war. They put him on a cocktail of drugs that basically numbed him out and he didn't feel anything for a while. He knew it wasn't the answer. He knew he had friends who had committed suicide while on the antidepressants that were meant to help them, some of which list "suicidal ideation" as a side effect.

Ben realized that medication wasn't helping him—the opposite—and he sought out other programs, one in Florida, another in Texas, and finally one in Ohio. That was the one that helped the most. He found the root cause of his depression—the childhood trauma of growing up in a dysfunctional family coupled with the moral injury from war itself. The counselors in the program taught him to see himself as being on a hero's journey and to make a container for his emotions. *At the end of my time there, I was able to let go of the hatred that I had for the individuals who tried to kill me. I felt love and compassion for the people who I had to engage with, who I had to kill to not be killed by, to not have my friends killed next to me. I was able to put myself in their shoes and realize that these poor young men in these third-world countries that are not very educated, they're me. I'm them. If I would've grown up where they grew up and was fed the propaganda that they were fed, I would've been fighting myself. I was able to come to peace with losing friends, being injured, wounded, medevaced overseas.*

But it wasn't soon enough to save his marriage. Ben and his wife are separated now. And Ben has been diagnosed with pre-Alzheimer's and dementia by his neurologist, from all the concussive blasts and explosions he experienced. He's on medications usually taken by people in their seventies and eighties. He's been working with a speech pathologist because he was having difficulty forming sentences. He thinks his brain began to atrophy from things like having his vehicle blown up by an RPG or being so close to an air-support mission where a 500-pound bomb was dropped.

Still, Ben wouldn't want to live anywhere else—despite everything he went through, despite Halliburton and the botched withdrawal from Afghanistan and the lies he was told and the injuries he's sustained, both physical and moral. *I feel like I won the lottery being born in this country. This is the best country on earth. The things we complain about are small things, the privileges of being such a wealthy nation and having some of the freedom that we have.*

For Ben, the American Dream is the potential for upward mobility based on hard work and homeownership. And he feels it is attainable for him; the obstacles stemmed from feelings of betrayal, from the decisions that were made, the *profits* that were made by contractors and government officials who sent him to fight their wars. *I would say the American Dream is still attainable, but it's incredibly difficult and becoming more difficult. It's very difficult for the general public to get honest information because there are so many unelected bureaucrats that have overreaching power that supersedes elected officials that are appointed. If a former director of the CIA can lie to Congress under oath and then apologize later, and after they get caught in these things, they just retire with all their benefits and connections and end up in the military-industrial complex side of it, it gets pretty dark, like we're not following our laws. A regular citizen is not going to just get away with an apology.*

To Ben, a crucial part of the American Dream is the consent of the governed, which means getting the truth from those in power. When the government lies so brazenly, like about the wars Ben fought, you can't really say that the citizenry, even people who are financially stable, are truly living the American Dream. The real betrayal is the decimation of the middle class and homeownership—connected in Ben's mind with the stability of our democracy, which relies on self-reliant citizens who are told the truth by their government. *If we're not careful, we could lose the soul of our country, what made it great to begin with, which was that it doesn't matter where you come from, the class you were born into, you can come here, you can be given a shot if you work hard. If you put forth the effort, you're going to be successful, you're going to be able to provide for your family and leave something to your descendants.*

———

Kevin Harper hasn't made it far geographically in the forty-six years he's lived on this planet. He was born and raised in Long Beach, California, and he now lives in Carson, just thirteen miles away. But economically, he's traversed the yawning divide separating the working poor from the stable middle class. He still can't quite see himself as middle class, though: *I would look at myself as working-to-middle class, because I am basically okay. I still have to work, but I'm in a little bit of a different situation than a lot of people. My wife has a decent job—together we gross about $130,000 a year. I live in a decent neighborhood. I have a pool in the backyard. I'm a homeowner. The cars are paid off. And I'm a retiree.*

Kevin spent twenty years in the military, and, in the beginning, it was a huge culture shock coming from Long Beach. He grew up on the edge of poverty, though unlike most families in the neighborhood, he grew up with a mom and a dad in the home. He had two dads, actually—his stepfather and his real father, who, even after he split from Kevin's mom, told Kevin, "Me and your mom aren't together, but I'm always here for you." His mother worked as a medical assistant, and his dad was a DJ. *He taught me fashion and all that stuff, but his type of job . . . it can get tight, and my mom's job didn't really pay that much, so we lived in apartments and things of that sort. I didn't like that, not because it was an apartment, but because you always felt poor. You always felt broke. Even as a kid, I was like, I don't want to be in that position. I don't want to be like this. I need to find a way to change that. And my way of doing that was by joining the military.*

Kevin knew that if he joined the military, he would get a college education, because the military promised to put you through college, and there was a good retirement. He thought he'd stay for the education and then get out, but he stayed for two decades and built a career there.

It wasn't easy at first for a Black kid from Long Beach. He had heard the *Dukes of Hazzard* theme song, but he'd never met anyone who really, *really* liked that song—who were *supporters* of that theme song. He had never seen people dip. He had never heard bluegrass. He had never been told to "turn that four-letter-word off" when playing rap music. Those first weeks, he thought he'd made a big mistake enlisting. But he got past those initial interactions and started making friends, and it turned out, those white friends *also* hated the *Dukes of Hazzard* guys who told Kevin to turn off his rap music. Kevin is still friends with some of them twenty years later; they turned out to be the most accepting people he's ever met. A white guy named Cruz and a Black guy from Compton named Kevin Nelson—the Kevin who would later go on to start Quality Cleaning Solutions—got Kevin through those early days—they stuck up for him and had his back.

He also met people who admitted to him that they were racist—something Kevin found fascinating, and he would always demand to know more. He wanted to understand why. They told Kevin, "I've never really seen Black people. I'm coming from a small town, it's about this big. The only Black people I see is on TV." *Until you meet a good Black person, you believe that they're all messed up. Until you meet a good white person, you believe that they might be racist. Then you're like, Oh man, it's not like that—at least, not with this person. There are situations you encounter, and it changes you. It changes the landscape of your personality and behavior and all that. One of the things that I noticed is, a lot of my Caucasian friends don't like when Black guys act like thugs. And then one of the things we don't like is when they act like they're better. You just have to figure it out. We all have to exist on the same planet. We're all gonna have things we don't agree with, but that doesn't mean you have to hate the person. There's always going to be differences in cultures and people, but you've got to learn to love what's good about people. Especially in the military, because when it comes down to it, are we together or are we apart? There's no room for anybody that's gonna be apart. They pretty much get weeded out. You have to know you've got that battle buddy.*

Kevin took advantage of every educational opportunity that presented itself and became a certified firefighter and an aviation boatswain's mate—one of the guys on the flight deck with the yellow float coats. And in the meantime, he got married to his wife, who he'd met back in Long Beach when they were kids but didn't start dating until he was in his mid-twenties, when they walked down the aisle as bridesmaid and groomsman at a friend's wedding. Kevin had been more of a party guy before that, out in the clubs chasing girls. Then one day when he was twenty-six, he was just done with all of that and ready to settle down. But even when he'd been living the fast life, he had been extremely careful not to have any kids before he got married. *That's one of the downfalls adults have. If you have a baby real early, you're already in a financial issue, especially if you're in high school, because you're not even working a real job. When you add a baby on top of that, which is a real financial responsibility, how much opportunity do you have to try to go out there and be successful? You're just trying to survive. It's strictly survival mode.*

There were a long of young parents in Long Beach—kids his age having kids. And it started early. *During high school, there were a couple, then a nice little surge around the age of nineteen, and after that, it just started spreading. Like, make it rain.*

Like Kevin, his wife was very driven to have a career. She had her first child just before meeting Kevin when she was twenty-five. Now she works as a manager for the Long Beach Parks and Recreation Department. They have three kids, and Kevin's family is the most important thing in his life.

After he got out of the military, he joined his military buddy Kevin Nelson in a cleaning business, but he stepped back after a few years. The market for cleaning businesses is severely undercut by illegal immigrants, who are willing to work for less than minimum wage, making the business an incredibly challenging one. It was taking a toll on his family. *To be financially successful without having the support of the people that are around—your family and all that—it's just not me, it's not something that I really entertain. I knew a gunnery sergeant when I used to be stationed in Key West who's retired now. He was a great guy. And he recently told me his son will not talk to him. His family is gone. He basically has nothing left except for his retirement check—and his ex-wife gets half of that. To me, that's like the worst thing that could happen: to finally make it to that goal of retirement, and then everything that you get it for is gone.*

But Kevin's not quite ready to call it quits yet. For now, he's doing gig-economy stuff, and he's looking for his next move, maybe something in housing development and management. It's not in his nature to kick back. It's in his nature to plan and execute.

He had to figure it out for himself, though, and it took twenty years. No one really explained to him growing up that there are keys to unlocking a successful life—things like planning, foresight, sacrifice, and hard work. You have to really want it, and no one can want it for you. Unfortunately, a lot of people don't learn these lessons in time. *Some people truly do not understand economic systems. They truly do not understand how to manage finances, if I don't pay my rent this month and I just stay here, they don't really understand what that's going to mean for the next episode that they have. How do you get to that point? It's that generational education. There's just certain things that aren't being taught, and you learn through life, and it's a repeat cycle that just keeps happening. And by the time you get it, you're in such a bad position, or you might've been locked up or whatever, it might be that it curbs the way that you can perform, and then it's hard for them to recover without them doing something else that's illegal.* He thinks one of the biggest things that would help the working class would be financial-literacy classes in high schools. Kids would definitely pay attention, and it would be a game changer for the working class.

Kevin's politics don't line up with either party. He thinks welfare creates dependency and doesn't think college should be free, but he supports universal health care and, on abortion, he thinks a woman should decide what happens to her body; if there's a victim at all, it's a father who might have wanted the baby. And he thinks people should spend a lot more time complaining about artificial intelligence taking people's jobs than illegal immigrants. *I'm kind of like a middle guy. Financially, I guess you could say I'm kind of like a Republican. But when it comes to human rights and stuff, there's some things that Democrats do have spot on. There's also some things that they're a little bit going crazy.* He thinks it's important to think for yourself. *Don't just be a Democrat because you grew up broke. Don't just be Republican because you came from a rural area. A lot of things that I learned when I was growing up about politics and stuff isn't necessarily correct.*

When it comes to achieving the American Dream, Kevin believes it takes a little good luck and a lot of hard work and foresight. If he had to sum it up, here's how he would put it: *You know the game is unfair, but you gotta play. You gotta find your own way to get through these barriers. Because if you don't figure it out, I don't think anybody's going to figure it out for you. You could go through life being mad about how things are unfair, or you could go and say, Hey, it's unfair, but I'm gonna go ahead and try to get it.*

The other day, his mom told him, "I'm so proud of you, you know that?" His father isn't the type to tell Kevin that he's proud of him, but recently he said, "You're doing good, son. Keep it up."

PART 2

How Can the Lives of Working-Class
Americans Be Improved?

INTRODUCTION
TO PART 2

Throughout the first part of this book, you read the stories of the kinds of people we never hear from—working-class Americans of all races, genders, creeds, ages, and geographic locations. You learned about their triumphs and sorrows, and how they view their shot at achieving some semblance of the American Dream. For many, the American Dream is already a reality. They have enough free time to pursue hobbies and spend time with family. Their children have the choice of going to college. They have savings put aside for emergencies and even retirement, or they have a pension that will ensure they can retire in dignity. Even their health-care costs are manageable.

Yet they are by no means the norm when it comes to the working class. They are in some ways a throwback to a time when being working class meant owning a home and having a pension and knowing your children would be better off. They are a crucial reminder that the American Dream is still achievable—and yet, so many Americans struggle to make it into the middle class.

Far more common are working-class Americans who work just as hard yet have no hope of homeownership or retirement owing to the cost of housing where they live and the cost of health care for nonunionized jobs. In a post-pandemic world where labor is scarce and a tight labor market has employers competing for workers, many workers are making more than they ever have before. And yet those hallmarks of a middle-class life—a home, upward mobility for your kids, affordable health care—still elude them, despite rising wages.

Then there are working-class Americans who just can't seem to get a solid footing and whose lives are beset by financial worry and despair.

What would help these people? How could we as a society make sure that more Americans are rising into the middle class and fewer sinking into poverty? Can the lives of working-class Americans be improved, and if so, how? Based on the challenges that working-class people identify as their primary barriers to the American Dream, are there policy solutions that are easy to identify and possibly not even that hard to implement that can help, and that working-class Americans would approve of? Can the American Dream be revived?

For most of the working-class people I spoke to for this book, the American Dream meant living a life free of economic instability and the kind of hopelessness it creates for people whose lives are never free from financial worry. Getting there for most of the people I interviewed involved owning a home or a piece of land, having wages that covered their bills with a little breathing room, and being able to save for retirement. When I asked people who had achieved these things how they managed, they talked about hard work, about being raised in families where their parents valued work and saw it not just in economic terms but almost spiritual ones. Working gives you self-esteem, gives you dignity. But they also all knew people who worked just as hard as they did yet found success elusive. Something I heard over and over sitting in people's living rooms and trucks and backyards during the past year was that you can do everything right and still only have a fifty-fifty chance of making it.

Still, a few themes did come up again and again. The cost of housing was a huge and constant theme in the interviews I did. Working-class Americans feel acutely the lack of housing in this country. Experts estimate the number of housing units we are short in the U.S. at between five and six million homes.

Another topic that came up repeatedly was immigration. Working-class Americans across the political spectrum felt strongly that mass immigration had contributed to lower wages for their work, worse conditions, and stiffer competition in general for lower-income people. People confessed this to me apologetically, assuring me they had nothing against immigrants. Indeed, many lived in immigrant communities, had immigrant friends and even family. But they felt that the devaluation of working-class jobs was tied to the lax border policy we've had over the last forty years.

Another big theme was the benefits cliff. People often told me that if you do everything right, the system somehow penalizes you. For example, unmarried mothers get a certain number of benefits, but if they meet someone and get married, or if they get a better job and get a raise, they lose those benefits, ending up in a much more precarious situation than where they started out.

And people felt acutely the absence of opportunities, of job training, and of good jobs where they lived.

I decided to go to the experts and ask them what solutions existed in these realms, and then to take the proposals back to the working-class Americans I'd interviewed to ask them what they made of them, which ideas they thought would most help them and the other struggling members of their community. Those are the conversations you will find in part 2.

CHAPTER 4

GOOD JOBS

Nicole Day has never found it hard to find a job—maybe because it was never an option not to. She has always worked hard to support herself and her son. She's been a bartender, an office manager, a babysitter, and a coordinator at a halfway house. But recently, she's found it impossible to find a *good* job. The good jobs demand a college degree, even for work that doesn't use any skills you'd pick up in college. It's happened more than once that she's been forced to train her replacement—because he had a college degree.

"If you don't have a college degree, you don't get as many opportunities," Nicole told me. "You know, I understand that, but at the same time, it's hard for people who are intelligent, who can bring something to the table, and we just don't get the opportunity as much as other people."

Nicole is the victim of the growing class divide that privileges the college educated in many ways, reserving the best opportunities for them even when the jobs themselves don't require a college degree. "People that don't have degrees, we don't get an opportunity to show what we can do or even get looked at, like, 'Hey, let's see what they can do,'" she told me. "Even if someone has been with a company for five or ten years and a position opens up, they normally hire outside of the company with someone that has a degree versus an employee that's been there for so long. We don't get the opportunity."

The diploma glass ceiling is real, and it's been exacerbated by the automation of recruiting that happens through hiring websites. And it's been a barrier for many of the working-class people I spoke to, even the most successful ones. Skyler Adleta, the Ohio electrician, came up against it at his first real job at a paint factory when a manager position opened up. He knew that all the managers at the factory had a college degree, but he also knew his bosses liked him and thought of him as a talented guy, and they'd even implemented some of his ideas about how to streamline the work. So he decided to apply for the management position.

He went to one of the executives and said, "Hey, I'm really interested in doing this. I don't have experience in management, but I have a rapport with all the guys, they know I work hard and you guys know I care because you've seen some of my ideas implemented. If there is even any chance, I'd like to be considered for this position."

But there was no chance. "You know it's company policy that these management level positions require a college degree," the executive told him.

"Okay. But do you think I could do it?" Skyler asked.

"As far as competence is concerned, absolutely," the executive admitted. "I think you'd be great at it. But I got a production floor of 200 employees. If I give you a management job over guys that have been here for twenty years, do you know what kind of morale issue I'm gonna have?"

"Or it could be the beginning of the guys who deserve opportunities to be encouraged that it's possible," Skyler countered.

"That's not what it's going to be," the executive said. "It's going to be 200 guys that are frustrated that someone who hasn't been here as long as them, who has just as little qualifications as them coming into a position that historically we haven't allowed them to even apply for."

"Well then, I'm not going to work here much longer," Skyler said.

"I don't want that to be how this conversation ends," the executive replied, but he wouldn't change his mind.

Skyler left a few weeks later for the trades, where a more merit-based system still prevails. Making the trades an attractive, viable, available option for more young Americans is one of the things I heard a lot while reporting this book. Vocational training in schools, for example, used to be a mainstay in this country. Eric, the Pittsburgh elevator electrician, remembers it well. "In my senior year, the carpentry class teacher would take you to take the union test for carpenters," he recalled. "They would get a van and they would rent it and they would take the whole class, whoever wanted to go to take the test." That was twenty-five, thirty years ago. It's unheard of now. "They don't do that no more. They don't promote the trades. And being a carpenter is a very good living. It ain't gonna make you rich, but it will keep you well off. You can make eighty grand a year. You can provide for your family decently."

What shifted in the intervening years was part of a national trend toward emphasizing college and the knowledge industry. This emphasis on college turned out to be little more than a sleight-of-hand to disguise the devastating impact globalization was having on the American working class. Language stressing meritocracy was once the hallmark of Republicans. "All Americans have the right to be judged on the sole basis of individual merit and to go as far as their dreams and hard work will take them," Ronald Reagan told members of his administration. But it became the go-to language for Democrats in the Clinton and Obama years, as Michael J. Sandel pointed out in *The Tyranny of Merit*. While actively promoting economic policies that shipped good-paying working-class jobs overseas, the Democrats' rhetoric shifted the blame to the workers themselves, as if it were a failure of natural talent and merit that was responsible for their downward mobility.

"In the old days, a young person, they might have just followed their parents' footsteps and gotten a job in their parents' line of work, keep that job for thirty, forty years," Obama told an audience at a Brooklyn technology college in 2013. "If you were willing to work hard, you didn't necessarily need a great education. If you'd just gone to high school, you might get a job at a factory, or in the garment district. You might be able to just get a job that allowed you to earn your wages, keep pace with people who had a chance to go to college. But those days are over, and those days are not coming back. We live in a twenty-first-century global economy," Obama went on, as though that economy were not built by his own party but rather an act of God. "And in a global economy, jobs can go anywhere. Companies, they're looking for the best-educated people, wherever they live, and they'll reward them with good jobs and good pay. And if you don't have a well-educated workforce, you're going to be left behind. If you don't have a good education, then it is going to be hard for you to find a job that pays a living wage."[1]

The message to working-class Americans wasn't just that they had missed the boat, but that it was their own stupidity and lack of education that resulted in the widening chasm separating them from the college educated, and that the college educated *deserved* their good fortune, for they had earned it with their studiousness.

That view very much trickled down to the working class. "You have a generation of young people who are taught that to end up in the working classes means missing the train," Skyler told me. "Essentially, if you don't go get a college degree, you're doomed or relegated to the lowest caste that exists in American society, which is the working class—or honestly, even more dehumanizing, the non-college-degreed class; I don't think they even called it anything. You're just doomed."

Contrary to what Presidents Clinton and Obama might have said, this didn't happen by magic; it was part and parcel of a very conscious effort by people in power to shift the economy toward knowledge-industry jobs. "Some of those jobs of the past are just not going to come back," President Obama told a steelworker in Indiana about disappearing blue-collar jobs. As a result, a premium started to get placed on a college degree, which reinforced the class divide when those jobs increasingly commanded soaring wages, while working-class labor was further devalued.

You ended up with one set of jobs—those that didn't require college—that was disappearing and whose wages were being slashed, and another set of jobs—those of the college educated— that was increasingly attracting the lion's share of the rewards. "And rather than try to do anything about this, policymakers basically doubled down on it and started to accelerate it," explains Oren Cass, founder and executive director of American Compass. "The theory was we're going to accelerate this and we're going to make everybody into a college graduate—look at these great jobs that the economy is creating! Let's just do everything we can to get the economy creating those great jobs, and then we'll somehow turn everybody into the kind of people who will do those great jobs. And that was a catastrophic failure—except for the segment of the population that does in fact complete college and goes on to do those jobs. The funny thing is that in a sense, our economic policy worked phenomenally well in delivering on the thing we said the goal was. We just had totally the wrong goal."[2]

The diploma divide ended up leaving behind two-thirds of the country, and that had a massive impact on the working class, but not just an economic one. The measure of your worth as an American became increasingly tied to your level of education. The dominant culture, once defined in a unifying way from the point of view of the lowest common denominator, came to be defined by people at the top. Sitcoms that were once about working-class families and procedurals about police detectives became shows about professional urban singles and FBI agents—distinguished from their police brethren by their college degrees. Elite tastes started to separate from the two-thirds of the nation without a college degree as those elites became so much richer. Then they took over the entertainment and media industries, from where they could define the values and the norms of the rest of the country. That created enormous downward pressure, not just economically but spiritually, too.

"The problem isn't that Jeff Bezos has a $500-million yacht," says Cass. "The problem is that the standards of what success looks like get defined by this upper-middle-class group that defines the culture and the media and so forth, and in consumer terms, it's the most profitable segment of the consumer market. The problem is when the restaurant you can afford to go out to to celebrate a special occasion becomes a punch line," one that's reiterated in every show and movie on your streaming service, written by members of the elite with an elite audience in mind, to whom Olive Garden or Dairy Queen is a joke. "That's a real problem. It's still the same restaurant you can afford to go to, but you no longer feel like you can participate in society and be proud of your achievements the way you may have in the past." The stories that we tell, that we present as success and the American Dream, have moved up with the upper middle class, even though the vast majority of the population is not there.

People benefiting from the diploma divide often talk about it in terms of merit like Obama did. But it's anything but. It's a caste system: you're born into a higher caste, your parents make sure you go to college, and you are ensured a much better life, irrespective of whether you're competent or not.

I asked Jim, a Brooklyn bartender, what the biggest impediment was to working-class Americans achieving the American Dream, and he thought for a minute before pinpointing a single factor: "The imbalance. The middle class is less than it was, and there seems to be upper-middle-class affluence that borders on elitism," he said. "Fifty, sixty years ago, you went to school and got a degree and were able to apply somewhere, and through your own efforts, you would work your way up." This is no longer the case. "To be middle class means to be on the level of the people that are upper middle class, that are highly affluent. The key is getting into a really good university, which doesn't matter much as far as your intellect is concerned. It's just a card you can show somebody else who's already there."

The diploma divide was further accelerated by something called "degree inflation"—when companies randomly require a college degree to even apply to a job, though that job doesn't require any skills learned in college. Degree inflation, which is rampant in the U.S., was the result of the offshoring of manu-facturing jobs, the automation of others, and the tech revolution, all of which shifted the focus of the economy away from jobs that rewarded brawn to jobs that involved long hours before a computer and softer, social skills. "As routine work became less common, a higher percentage of jobs entailed significant social interaction," write Joseph B. Fuller and Manjari Ramen in a 2017 report for Harvard Business School called "Dismissed by Degrees."[3] "Employers increasingly expected middle-skills workers, like IT help-desk technicians, salespeople, and nursing aides, to possess a range of soft skills, such as the ability to handle interpersonal interaction and work in team settings, flexibility, and problem-solving."

As a result, between 2010 and 2016, only one job out of every 100 new jobs created was open to a worker with a high-school degree or less, and of the eleven million jobs created during those six years, three out of four required a bachelor's degree or more.

One thing that can be done to immediately reverse this dev-astating trend is to eliminate college requirements for jobs that don't actually require a college education. Such an effort is actually underway, though not to the extent that it should be. Mired in a post-pandemic labor crunch, companies have started eliminating degree requirements in order to attract more applicants. Walmart is perhaps the premiere example of this trend. Seventy-five percent of managers at Walmart are hired from within the ranks of store associates, and that includes higher-level managers. "There are many roles in the U.S. job market, especially in the service sector, where a college degree should not be required for career access and mobility. For example, we do not require Walmart store managers, who earned average total compensation of approximately $230,000 in FY2023, to have a college degree," according to Walmart's website. And for jobs that require a specific skill set you learn in college, Walmart will pay for its workers to go to college. Walmart has also "banned the box" where people who served time in prison have to inform their employer on a job application.

Some states are getting rid of degree requirements. Pennsylvania, Utah, Colorado, and Maryland have eliminated four-year college degree requirements from the majority of government jobs, and Georgia and Alaska are following suit, opening up thousands of jobs to people who had been barred from them for administrative reasons, reversing the recent trend of randomly listing a college degree as a requirement and locking two-thirds of Americans out of jobs that don't need a college education.

I asked Nicole if she thought that would help—companies getting rid of degree requirements for positions that don't really utilize skills you learn in college. "I really, really think it would in a lot of cases," she told me. "I'm not saying every case is the same. Obviously, every company is different and there's different positions for each company. I just feel like there would be a little more opportunity. I always hear 'You're never too old to go back to school,' and I get that, but I can't put my life on hold for four-to-eight hours a day, try to go to school and get all these student loans and debts that I'm not gonna be able to pay back." And it's especially unfair because Nicole has something a recent college grad doesn't. "I have way more experience than someone that has a college degree, but I don't have that piece of paper to show that employer that I have that college degree. Ten years' experience at that job doesn't matter."

It's not just about getting rid of a college degree. It's also about training Americans for the kinds of jobs for which there simply aren't enough workers. There is a huge deficit of skilled tradesmen in this country, while millions of working-class people are desperate for good jobs. Vocational training in high schools, once a staple of the American educational system, would go a long way to matching workers with jobs. Wherever working-class life is thriving in the U.S., you can find a local investment in vocational training. But it's the exception, not the rule. Federal and state governments give a total of $150 billion every year to fund higher education—compared to a measly $1 billion to Career and Technical Education.[4] And this despite the fact that careers that require a college degree are all in decline, whereas there is a huge shortage of workers who are skilled in the trades or who work in growing industries like the service industry.

One of the things that draws workers to Las Vegas is the Culinary Academy of Las Vegas, a joint venture of employers— casinos like MGM, Caesars, and the Wyn—and the Culinary Workers Union coming together to set up a training ground so that workers get the skills they need to succeed in the work-force. They graduate and are immediately hired to union positions—often at the graduation ceremony itself, where managers from the casinos hover like vultures to pluck their next crop of workers. They stand at the back of the room waiting for the ceremony to end so they can offer people jobs, and sometimes they will approach students' family members to make the pitch. The

Culinary Academy graduates between 1,500 and 2,000 students a year, of whom more than 80 percent qualify for tuition assistance, and they have a 92 percent job-placement rate. They figured out that sending people out to find their own scholarships meant they were losing students, so they brought in an in-house social services team with a licensed social worker, who sits down with new students as soon as they arrive and asks them, "Tell me where you've been, tell me your job history, tell me where you want to be in terms of your career." If they need it, she gives them a bus pass, or if they need help getting SNAP benefits while they are in school, she'll help with that, too. The Culinary Academy will do anything to get students through that three-week or three-month course, because they know there's a job waiting for them at the end—a good union job that pays more than $20 an hour and has comprehensive health care. Every single student files three job applications before they finish, but most have a job already lined up by the end. The career developer has connections will all the recruiting agencies, and they will often call and say, "Hey, I have five openings, do you have any students?" Or she'll call and say, "Hey, I've got three students, what are you looking for?"

A lot of the students are fresh out of high school, but there are also people just looking for a good job with no experience in hospitality who need skills. But half of their students are union workers looking to upskill and retrain for even better positions. Their benefits package includes full tuition for any training they want to do, and the Culinary Academy creates class schedules around their work schedule, so they don't have to miss work and wages.

The Culinary Academy has three tracks: culinary, food and beverage, and housekeeping. The campus itself has a café, where students in the barista training program brainstorm their own espresso concoctions—butter latte, London fog tea latte, marble mocha—and then prepare them for the academy's staff, who

can buy coffee drinks. It also has a full kitchen and on-site restaurant, where front and back of the house can train, and it has
mock hotel rooms for the big casinos—Caesar's Palace, MGM,
Wyn—set up with all the fixings: a king-size bed, a couch, a TV
and dresser, and an en-suite bathroom, so room attendants can
walk into their jobs on Day One with something familiar to greet
them. The hotels all refresh their rooms regularly, and they will
donate their old linens and furniture to the academy so they can
keep current. And each has its own layout. Caesar's, for example,
has a specific pillow layout, which the instructor is familiar with,
so she can come to the Caesar's Palace room and ask, "Is the bed
skirt where it needs to be? Is the runner where it needs to be?
Did you get all the surfaces?" And if a student can't finish the
room in the amount of time necessary, they usually just need a
few more days to run through it, get the memorization down.
Instructors will come through and dirty up the rooms and the
floors, and then teach students the best chemicals for cleaning
specific stains. They also let filmmakers use the rooms because
there's a lot less red tape than filming in a hotel, and they feed
fifteen veterans lunch and dinner every Monday, Wednesday,
and Friday because their veterans' home doesn't have a kitchen.
There is also a special program for integrating students with
disabilities like developmental disabilities into the program and
finding ways for them to excel.

All the time spent on campus is part of the training, so students have to be in a clean, pressed uniform while on campus
and have to enter through the back door, just like they will at the
casinos. It's all part of making sure they will succeed by helping
them be prepared for the workforce.

Others have taken up the mantle of vocational training on
their own, as a private initiative. After a career spent in janitorial
services, Earl Burnett has become a professional mentor. Based
in Riverside, California, Earl's black hair and beard are now gray,

framing shining dark skin that's barely lined at all. He wears thin, wire-rimmed glasses and has a wide, open smile that's impish despite his advancing years, and ready to split open any doorway that might think itself closed.

Earl never had trouble finding work, but he found his calling after meeting a guy who owned a janitorial business and was making good money. Earl started following his wife Virginia around the house, watching her as she cleaned, taking notes. When he explained what he was doing, Virginia wasn't sure how she would feel about telling people her husband cleaned toilets. She did a lot of praying on it and finally landed on something her mom told her after she and Earl first got married: "Whatever he wants to do, as long as it's positive and gonna benefit you and your family, you ride with it."

Earl bought a vacuum cleaner and went out in search of contracts. He knew the ticket to his success would be how thorough he was, so he brought Virginia in at first, along with a few women from the church. He wanted to learn how to have a woman's touch. He wanted to see what women saw. One day he asked Virginia, "Babe, when you go in the bathroom and you sit down, what do you see?"

"I ain't trying to see nothing!" she replied.

But he learned the difference between women's and men's bathrooms quickly, which helped him understand what he wanted his signature touch to be. He started to learn how different cleaning products cleaned differently, and after a while, it just snowballed. He got a lot of compliments on his bathrooms, and a lot of callbacks. "You win a contract or lose a contract in the bathroom," Earl explained to me. "'This man can clean a bathroom,' they said. And then the contracts started rolling in." *That's my niche*, Earl decided. Handling stool was at first very difficult for him, until it hit him: Spray the stool. Then it's like mud. "I can handle mud. Okay, cool. I can handle that now."

Pretty soon, Earl's cleaning business was a success. He remembers calling his father to tell him the first time he made $25 an hour—his father who was eighty at the time and had made $25 a week for much of his life. "Son, I should come work for you," Earl's father replied proudly.

Twenty-five years later, Earl still has his own cleaning company with some big-name contracts, including Enterprise rentals, which allows Earl to subcontract out to other small business owners. He doesn't choose them at random; they are young up-and-coming small business owners whom Earl mentors. He teaches classes on how to start your own janitorial business, how to excel at cleaning, how much to charge, what the best products are. But he still loves the cleaning part of the job. He loves when a plan comes together. He loves restoring order. He loves making good decisions about which materials to use and how to treat them. He loves the perfection at the end.

But he also teaches the business side of things: Don't chase the money. Know your value. Don't work for less than you want to be making. Hustling is good but repeat business is how you're going to sustain yourself—repeat business and referral business. Which means don't be in a rush. Put in the time, give every case the attention it deserves. Stay focused.

He's given his course to young Black business owners, to veterans, to at-risk youth. He's been hugely successful in his community, changing the lives of countless new small business owners. He taught one class to fourteen men who had recently been released from prison. The minimum sentence served among them was thirty-eight years. He taught them everything he knew about business, had them come up with names for their businesses and design a logo and then surprised them by printing the logos and their names on business cards. There were a lot of hardened men holding back tears the day he gave out the business cards.

But like so many other things, vocational training doesn't exist in a vacuum. "I think that vocational training is very good, but you have to think about what vocations are going to continue to exist that something like AI or a robot can't do in the future, versus the stuff where they're going to let the genie out of the bottle and be like, oops, sorry, none of you have jobs, we've got this robot to do your job—do you want to invest in a robot?" Jamie, the Home Depot manager from Vermont, told me. "In general, vocational training is very good—a way better solution than college, in my opinion, at this point for the average American. An electrician is typically much more financially successful than somebody who studied earth science at college and got a master's degree."

In the face of the diploma divide, progressives have called for a $15 minimum wage, which would significantly raise the country's current $7.25 an hour. This was one of the main campaign promises of progressive standard-bearer Senator Bernie Sanders during his two presidential campaigns, and the Service Employees International Union's Fight for $15, which brought together workers from a number of fast-food chains to demand higher wages. The Fight for $15 had a big impact: New York, Seattle, California, Florida, New Jersey, and Nebraska are among the states that have signed a $15 minimum wage into law or are in the process of doing so. Of all the states in the union, just five don't have a minimum wage, while two have a minimum wage below the federal minimum. At the same time, wages for the vast majority of Americans have begun to eclipse even $15 an hour.

Of the people I interviewed, a few outright opposed the idea of a $15 minimum wage, like Jamie, who felt it destroyed entry-level positions for young people. "Why would a place hire an eighteen-year-old to push carts if they could hire a twenty-five- or thirty-year-old who is generally more mature and settled? It sounds callous in today's environment, but I think competition is a good thing and the higher the minimum wage gets, the closer we get to socialism," he told me.

But most of the opposition I encountered was due to $15 an hour not being nearly enough to live on. Most people I interviewed were incredulous trying to picture how anyone could make it on less than that, especially with prices what they are. "Poverty is statistically simple: People are poor because they're paid poorly. That's it," Cyrus, the Phoenix Medicare Advantage customer service rep, told me, when I flew out to Phoenix to interview him, and we spent a few days driving his route as a former trucker—the gas stations he'd brought fuel to and the pot farms he'd delivered CO_2 to. "There's not a politician in this country that would go on record and say, 'You have to work more than forty hours a week to rent an apartment.' They're not gonna say that." Yet they won't insist that workers be paid a living wage. "When you go pick up your groceries and go to check out, do you know if that checkout girl has a roof over her head? That's the country I want to live in. The moment you start going into the repercussions of poverty wages, that's when you get into a white-paper conversation about all these random, admin-heavy solutions that have nothing to do with the underlying problem, which is if you increase the wage, housing follows and then society follows. Depression gets alleviated. It is crippling to be poor—psychologically, spiritually, physically. It destroys the body. And it destroys the soul. Since the majority of Americans can actually work, you raise the wage and shut the f--- up. It's a silver bullet."

"I'm not too big on the government forcing people to do certain things, because I think that's a slippery slope," Kevin Nelson, the California janitor, told me. "But I do think that because we live in a society of capitalism, that could create greed, and you know the condition of our country—wages is a huge issue. Maybe we as people have gotten so greedy that we forgot about our fellow man, and the government does have to step in. But I don't think the minimum wage we have now is sufficient. You have people making $17 an hour and they can't pay their rent."

While people hated the idea of someone putting in a full day's work and still being broke at the end of it, there was skepticism that a national minimum wage was the solution. Not only is $15 or $16 an hour short of what would sustain a family, but it didn't seem to offer a path upward toward self-sufficiency, economic stability, and most importantly, opportunity—which is what people were really after.

"I think the minimum-wage discussion is looking at things from the wrong end," Gord, the Ithaca truck driver, told me. "Why are we not talking about either reforming or dismantling systems that channel so much money to the top and away from the bottom, and removing people's opportunity and creating all these stratified systems that don't change very often and then make people more poor? That strikes me as a more useful endeavor than having the government come in and carpet bomb everybody with minimum wages that may or may not work." Those systems include things like credentialism, a ballooning government bureaucracy, and the skyrocketing cost of a home—things it's very much not in the interests of people in power to fix.

But actually, wherever you look there are small ways to fix what ails working-class life, only no one will do anything about it. "Where I'm coming from in the trucking business, I've been in it long enough now that I can see how certain tweaks would benefit most truckers greatly," Gord told me. "But that tweak might add a marginal cost per trailer-load to Amazon that might make each load on average another fifty or sixty bucks more, or it might incentivize certain parts of the business to be more efficient, thereby allowing guys to make more money. But man, trying to get those tweaks done . . . There's an entire army of lobbyists and government people who are just trapped by their own inertia that this minor little tweak you could do to fix something is just impossible to get done."

One of those tweaks is the Guaranteeing Overtime for Truckers Act, a bill introduced into Congress that Gord has written about at a Substack he started to call attention to the challenges of the trucking industry. Truckers are exempted from overtime pay, and many of them are paid by the mile, which means they spend a lot of time at work not getting paid. The bill would rectify that, and make it illegal to deprive truckers overtime pay. "I cannot express to you enough what a fundamental change that would have for the trucking industry, because it's built around driver's time not being paid for," Gord told me, and started listing them off: "All the inefficiencies of time loading and unloading. Drivers feeling like they gotta work their asses off because they're only getting paid by the mile and we get delayed everywhere. It would go a long way toward solving safety problems. It would go a long way toward improving drivers' wages. It would go a long way through toward improving the efficiency of the supply chain. That one tweak would be a game changer for the trucking business." Yet the bill has languished in committee and no one with the power to push it through seems at all interested in doing so.

When we checked in a few months later, Gord had been laid off from his trucking job. The bottom has fallen out of the hardwood market, especially the international market. China and Vietnam aren't buying as much, and lumber just isn't moving, so the price for standing timber is in the toilet, which means landowners aren't selling their trees and there's no work for Gord hauling logs. To pay his bills, Gord has been doing construction work for his brother-in-law, and he's considering an electrical apprenticeship. He's forty-four, so if he's going to make a career change, it's got to be soon. But he plans to keep a foot in both camps. "In my heart, I'm a trucker," he told me. "It's in my blood. I'll always be one. Maybe I'll work part-time, do the odd trip here and there."

Like the trades, manufacturing, too, used to be a source of stability and upward mobility for millions of American workers, until disastrous globalization efforts took an ax to that whole sector, shipping up to five million good-paying jobs that secured a middle-class life to Mexico and China, and leaving the communities that were once anchored around those jobs flailing and descending into miasmas of despair.

Those jobs were sent overseas thanks to ruinous trade deals signed into law over the past thirty years. Those deals have undeniably raised our GDP in the aggregate. And yet, the rewards of that have gone almost exclusively to the top 20 percent while devastating the working class, and not just from an economic point of view.

Economists have found again and again that free trade and the opioid crisis feed each other.[5] One study found that for every 1,000 people who lost their jobs in a county, there was a 2.7 percent rise in opioid-related overdose deaths.[6] A Yale study from 2020 found the same thing: areas exposed negatively to international trade policy experienced an increase in fatal drug overdoses, specifically in the white population.[7] Once fentanyl entered the market, the same 1,000 trade-related job losses led to an 11.3 percent spike in overdose deaths.

But the government can just as easily choose to create policy that protects the working class as it has chosen to make policy that hurts the working class. Steel is a great example of that. In 2018, President Trump imposed massive tariffs on steel and aluminum imports, meaning that if you were a company that needed steel and you bought your steel from China, you were going to have pay 25 percent more than if you bought your steel from an American producer. President Biden has so far held the line on those tariffs, despite the World Trade Organization denouncing them as a violation of international trade rules. Tariffs on steel are a big part of why the average steel mill worker makes $88,000 a year—a middle-class wage in many parts of the country.[8]

Contrary to what President Obama believed, you *can* protect good, working-class jobs. You *can* bring these jobs back. You *can* reverse the perverse incentive to send everyone to college. We can have an industrial policy that encourages people to bring back manufacturing. There are many ways the government can help incentivize businesses to stay in the U.S., to build in the U.S., to produce in the U.S., to hire in the U.S. Like immigration and offshoring, our trade policies are a choice made by the government. Just as the government can encourage trade policies that help the working class, they can encourage the reshoring of manufacturing with policies like the CHIPS and Science Act, which earmarked $50 billion to create semiconductor factories here in the U.S.

Whether it's in manufacturing, the trades, health care, or the service industry, working-class Americans want *good jobs* with opportunity for growth that provide the kinds of stability that we all seek for ourselves and our families. The answers for how to approach financial policy in a way that stabilizes America and helps the working class achieve a middle-class life are there, if only our politicians want to enact them.

CHAPTER 5

WHOSE JOBS?

Corrie Zech, who you met in Chapter One, leans more toward the liberal side of things. She believes housing should be guaranteed by the government—an idea she knows is unpopular in suburban Ohio where she lives, where most people are more conservative. But there are a few issues where she agrees with her family and neighbors, and chief among them is immigration.

It came up when I asked Corrie how she would define the American Dream. "I believe it exists for immigrants to this country, but for Americans themselves, I don't think it really exists much anymore," she told me. "It seems much easier for someone who comes into the country to get access to the resources needed to build whatever it is they're trying to build, whether it's come in and build a business or whatever. But it seems like for average Americans to get access to those resources is 10,000 times harder than it would be for someone else."

"Why is that?" I asked.

"I wish I had an answer for that," Corrie said. "I don't have a good answer for it. I believe people can really achieve what they put their minds to. But it's been my experience that the people who try the hardest seem to have the toughest time getting the things that they need."

Immigration was one of the topics that most united the working-class people I spoke to, and most divides people at the top of the income distribution from the working class. When educated Americans talk about illegal immigrants, they talk about them in moral terms, as refugees with asylum cases. Incapable of imagining themselves facing the desperation that would drive them to cross a desert and illegally enter another country, they feel sorry for illegal immigrants and feel a moral duty to accommodate them. But working-class Americans can very easily put themselves in the shoes of someone who might be driven to illegally cross a border out of economic desperation, someone just looking for a better life for their children. The absence of a yawning gap between themselves and poor migrants means there's no gap to fill with patronizing pity. Instead, they feel real empathy but also real frustration with the policies they feel favor people not too different from themselves when their own needs are pressing, and their own children's futures are in no way assured.

"As a man, how do you tell another man not to do everything he can to take care of himself and take care of his family and go where those opportunities lie at?" Kevin Nelson, the California janitor, told me. "Where it does become a problem is you have people who take lower wages, because they come from places where they're used to making very little." It's at the bottom end of the wage spectrum where illegal immigration has had the most ruinous impact, driving down wages and making businesses like Kevin's in cleaning services nearly impossible to sustain while paying workers a living wage, simply because there is so much low-wage competition. Kevin tries to combat that downward pressure with a value-add—by having the best equipment and a heat treatment method that is unique to him. But his former partner, Kevin Harper, came to believe that the sheer number of available migrants working for less than minimum wage would ultimately make their business unsustainable.

Because working-class Americans are doing jobs that immigrants compete for at the lower end of the wage market, they don't see the difference between themselves and illegal migrants in terms of economic status; their own precariousness gives them a feeling of kinship with illegal migrants. They certainly don't see it in racial terms, as some in the media would have you believe. The American working class is extremely racially diverse. Working-class Americans see the difference between themselves and illegal immigrants as a difference of citizenship. They are American, and they think that should mean something. They are frustrated when it seems like the opposite is true: immigrants are getting help they could desperately use and can't access.

This is why the topic of immigration comes up in places you might not expect, like when you ask people about the American Dream. It came up when I asked Jim, the Brooklyn bartender, what it means to him to be an American one afternoon. "It's hard to say because I don't know what it's like to be anything else," he told me. "The question probably would be, how would you feel if you were an immigrant coming over the border, being resented by the people that are here. It's a very convoluted thing. What am I looking at? Do I hate everybody? No. Is the world out of balance a little? Yeah. Are we a catchall for everybody? Apparently, we are. Can we tolerate it? Probably we can. Should we have to? I don't know. What if what you work for your whole life is going to deteriorate?"

It came up again when I asked Jamie, the Home Depot manager, to define the American Dream. "To me the American Dream is—and I just want to preface this: I am not anti-immigration whatsoever," Jamie told me. "The country exists because of immigration. And even the first settlers were immigrants. And you could even argue the American Indians at one point, they think they may have crossed the Bering Strait up to North America. So America has always been an immigration point and I understand that, and that is part of the charm of the United States—the diversity of thought and culture. So I just want to say that in the first place. But to me, the American Dream is that all citizens—

which is important—no matter what race, color, creed, they all have the equal opportunity to the promise, which was life, liberty, and pursuit of happiness."

Often, it was the empathy working-class Americans feel for immigrants—much more immediate than what the educated elites feel—that gave them the sense that the immigrants coming here, both legally and illegally, are doing so at their expense, taking something they feel was promised to them as Americans yet has not been delivered. Now that promise is being given to someone else, someone else's children—someone they wished well and had no ill will toward and yet whose improving circumstances they couldn't help but compare with their own feeling of losing ground, moving backward. Rather than talking about immigration in moral terms, they talked about it in economic terms, how it creates downward pressure on their wages, and more pressure on the markets for things they desperately need, like housing.

"I'm not anti-immigration," Gord, the Ithaca truck driver, told me over beers at his favorite local Ithaca brewery on a warm day in May. "The problem is you have to acknowledge the economic realities that come with that. And if you talk about it, they just say, 'Oh, you're racist.' It's like, no: More people means less real estate and higher prices. Can we at least acknowledge that that's happening—and that that means my children are going to have a harder time buying a house when they're older. *I'm* having a hard time buying a house now. Just admit that! They won't. What do you do with people that won't acknowledge reality? I don't know what to say to them."

Gord paused, took a swig of his beer and squinted. "You look really serious and you're drinking too slow," he scolded me and laughed. "You keep asking me if I have a message, and it's great to have a message. But it's better if someone is actually listening! And they don't."

The feeling that no one is listening came up again and again. At a McDonald's in Brooklyn across the street from the Family Dollar store where she worked, Lucia told me the same thing over iced coffee one afternoon in July: No one is listening, and there is no difference between the two political parties. "It's out of control," Lucia told me. "Everyone is running here to achieve the American Dream, and I just feel like, how can you promise this to other people when you can't even take care of the ones that you have here? *We* have homelessness. *We* have crime. *We* have poverty. And yet, we keep bringing more. Don't get me wrong," she added quickly. "They deserve that. They deserve the right to freedom. But it's like my mother always said: Don't go sticking your nose in nobody else's backyard when your backyard is not clean. We can't clean our own backyard. How do we help others? We can't help the ones we got here. We have veterans who risked their lives who are homeless. Why is that? Why do we have homeless veterans on the street in this country? They risked their lives for our freedom, but we can't feed them? We can't house them? But yet, we'll bring other people. And they don't understand why people are angry. I understand. I understand the hostility. I also think people deserve the right to freedom—but it's got to come from somewhere. It comes from us! You got to take care of us! You got to take care of us *first*. We were born here. So that's my issue. And it doesn't matter if you're Republican or Democrat."

Of course, not everyone agrees—like Colissa, the Georgia teacher. "Let the weary come," she told me. "How dare this country have a problem with immigrants coming when we are a nation of immigrants? I feel like a lot of the immigrants that come work so much harder, and they take jobs that Americans do not want. I'm not going out picking no oranges. I don't want to be a household maid. I don't want to go to work in a restaurant. I don't want to wash dishes. And you know, so many immigrants come and make their own businesses. I grew up in a neighborhood where all our corner stores were run by people from the Middle East."

Yet, as civil rights commissioner Peter Kirsanow told the Senate Subcommittee on Immigration in 2016, "illegal immigration has a disproportionately negative effect on the wages and employment levels of blacks, particularly black males." A 2008 briefing to the United States Commission on Civil Rights found that immigration is responsible for 40 percent of the decline in Black employment between 1960 and 2000 and has robbed American workers of $100 billion a year in wages, and even contributed to the Black incarceration rate. The briefing notes that "illegal immigrants and blacks (who are disproportionately likely to be low-skilled) often find themselves in competition for the same jobs, and the huge number of illegal immigrants ensures that there is a continual surplus of low-skilled labor, thus preventing wages from rising."[1] Unsurprisingly, immigration raids result in locally rising wages for Black workers.[2] "People often say, 'Well, illegal immigrants are taking jobs that Americans do not want to do. No one wants to be a hewer of wood or a drawer of water,'" writes Kirsanow. "The problem is that there are thousands of Americans, and always will be thousands of Americans, who find that those jobs are the only ones for which they are qualified. How can you better yourself if you cannot even get on the first rung of the employment ladder and find yourself essentially shut out of certain industries?" There is naturally a correlation between lower wages, higher unemployment, higher incarceration rates, and the breakdown of the Black family, with awful consequences for children. "The dearth of job opportunities gives these men less confidence in their ability to support a family, and gives women reason to fear that these prospective husbands will be only another mouth to feed," writes Kirsanow.[3] "Continuing to have high levels of low-skilled immigration, legal or illegal, will only further harm African-American workers. Granting legal status to illegal immigrants will be particularly harmful. Not only will the low-skilled labor market continue to experience a surplus of workers, making it difficult for African-Americans to find job opportunities, but African-Americans will be deprived of one of their few advantages in this market."

One of the most pro-immigration people I interviewed was also one of the most conservative—Skyler Adleta, the Ohio electrician. But even his view was very nuanced. "No, the border should not be open," he told me in his kitchen over iced tea and a Memorial Day spread that his wife Lauren had put out for us and their family friends. "There needs to be controlled immigration. However, what people can't forget is that if immigrants are willing to go through the process of coming into this country, I think America would be shooting itself in the foot to not accept the brightest and the best."

From Skyler's point of view, the skilled trades have been so degraded that there is just a huge dearth of labor, and one he can't imagine being adequately filled absent a huge, drastic push. "There's this general spirit among most of the working class that's like, we don't want these immigrants taking our jobs. But *you're* not even taking the jobs," Skyler pointed out. "And if you set aside the socioeconomic anxieties of the working class, we're going to reach a moment where we can't support infrastructure. We're not going to be able to continue to develop the way we have in the past couple hundred years, because no one's doing it, and I don't think technology is going to be able to fill the gaps, at least anytime soon."

I asked Skyler if he thought mass immigration was undercutting wages. "I don't have enough of an understanding to have a viable opinion on that," he said. "But what I would say is, in construction, I've seen crews that are staffed by illegal immigrants and they're not paying them an American wage by any stretch of the imagination. So those people in those roles are undercutting wages, yes. But the skilled trades are pretty well protected from a general laborer coming in and taking their job. A legal immigrant going through the preestablished apprenticeship program that's required for skilled trades, I don't know if it would affect that as greatly. Maybe if there was an oversaturation that occurred from it, economically that would happen."

"But you're saying we're very far from that?" I asked.

"We're very far from that."

The feeling of sympathy for immigrants but frustration with those in power—in both parties—for not caring about American workers is pervasive in the working class. People feel angry that they've been put in a position of competing for scraps at the bottom of the income distribution with desperate people, people with whom they inherently empathize. They are angry that people at the top are benefiting from the situation, or taking tax dollars and giving them to causes that have no connection to the working class. It's especially hard to see their tax dollars going to other countries, when so many here are in need.

It came up while driving with Amy, the Florida nurse's aide, in her SUV between her nursing home job and the second job she picked up to supplement her health care. "I don't think we should let them all in. Do I think we should let some in, as we used to a long time ago? I do," Amy told me. "I think people are just trying to survive, just trying to make it, take care of their kids. I feel so bad for 'em. I also know that we can only do so much [...]. But why can't we go over there, of course with their government's approval, and try to help them build their country? You know this whole marijuana legalization thing? Why can't we try to eliminate the cartels and build the factories over there? That would build up their country and they would stop coming over here. I mean, we're helping Ukraine fight this huge, massive war, but yet we're not allowed to help the people that are practically butted up against us, we're making them suffer, arresting them, separating their families, some of them come here and get threatened."

People in the media and politics on the right and the left often say that immigrants come here and work jobs that Americans don't want to do. But Skyler and Colissa were the only people I interviewed who agreed. Skyler felt that most Americans hadn't experienced the kind of desperation that many immigrants have, which makes them more willing to do low-skilled labor. Everyone else I interviewed felt like the problem wasn't the jobs themselves—none of which they felt were inherently undignified—but rather, the working conditions, the pay, the lack of adequate health care, and the inability to retire that made certain jobs unappealing.

The elites of both parties imagine that no one would want a job cleaning toilets or changing adult diapers, picking crops, or driving a truck and loading and unloading a haul, because they themselves would feel humiliated doing such "dirty" jobs. But this says more about the elites than anything else. Millions and millions of Americans—people like Elena and Gord and Earl and Amy find dignity in this labor. What lack of dignity exists is in the conditions of workplaces that don't pay well or protect their workers or offer a pathway to a dignified retirement.

And yet, it's undeniable that a glut of immigration over the past forty years—both legal and illegal—has made these jobs more precarious, less secure, less remunerative, and less dignified overall. Certainly, the existence of millions and millions of undocumented immigrants without worker protections who are willing to work for less than minimum wage keeps wages low for working-class Americans competing for those same jobs at minimum wage or higher. Meanwhile, visa programs for skilled workers create competition for trade work, and for some tech jobs. Companies would have to train Americans to do those jobs if they couldn't get workers from other countries for cheaper.

Immigration was one of the first topics where I noticed the class divide. Like many of the people I spoke to for the book, I live in an immigrant community. My father is an immigrant. My husband is an immigrant. At least half of my friends are immigrants. As a Jewish American, I feel keenly the debt I owe American immigration policy because it helped my ancestors escape the pogroms and persecution of the Old Country and find safe harbor in this, the greatest, most tolerant nation on earth. There was a time—I blush when I think about it—when I, too, called a dear friend xenophobic in a group email for suggesting we limit immigration.

And yet, the facts don't lie: immigration, especially the kind of mass immigration we've had in the past forty years has been extremely punishing to those in the working class, part of a dark brew of factors that have reduced their economic prosperity and cut them out of the American Dream. When elites call people racist for opposing immigration, they are doing so from a very unique position of privilege, having been the beneficiaries of mass immigration, in a very real, economic way, while the working class has paid for it. The rise in GDP that economists attribute to immigration is real—but it magically found its way to the top 10 percent, while everyone else was experiencing the opposite impact.

You can see this by comparing the stagnation of working-class wages with the number of immigrants entering the U.S. Back in 1970, the high-water mark for working-class wages, immigrants represented just 4.7 percent of the total U.S. population. Today, immigrants account for 13.7 percent of the U.S. population—closing in on the highest it's ever been, in 1890—which coincided with The Gilded Age, another period characterized by extreme inequality, as you can see in figure 9.[4]

Immigrants now account for 19 percent of workers overall, but the number is much higher for low-wage workers: Immigrants are 32 percent of workers making less than $30,000, compared

Figure 9. Immigrant Share of U.S. Population Nears Historic High

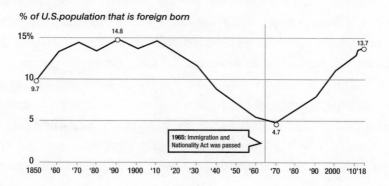

% of U.S.population that is foreign born

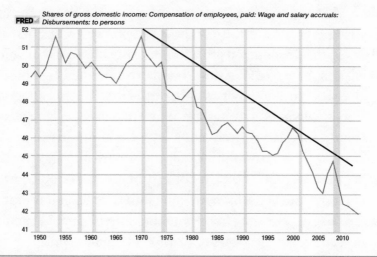

Shares of gross domestic income: Compensation of employees, paid: Wage and salary accruals: Disbursements: to persons

On the *top*, you can see the rising share of the immigrant population of the U.S. From the Pew Research Center. On the *bottom*, you can see the declining share of GDP that is made up of wages. Prepared by the Federal Reserve of St. Louis with data from the U.S. Bureau of Economic Analysis.

to just 16 percent of workers making more than $60,000 a year, meaning the pressure that immigrant workers are putting on the labor market is twice as great for lower-income Americans than it is for higher-income ones.[5] And because these numbers are from the United States Census, you can be sure they are undercounting the impact of illegal immigration on the labor market, as Oren Cass points out.[6]

"Immigration has provided the margin between a labor market in which employers would feel constant pressure to find and retain workers—especially lower-wage ones—and the labor market as it has operated, in which they can offer the same low wages and poor conditions for decades on end," writes Cass.[7]

It's this rise in mass immigration that's been left out of the story of stagnating working-class wages, though it's something working-class Americans are acutely aware of. Yet when people object to this level of mass immigration, they are often called racist, creating a taboo around the topic. Until President Trump made immigration a cornerstone of his campaign, both Republicans and Democrats had an agreement around lax immigration policy that favored amnesty and overall *more* immigrants.

In fact, the unspoken truth about immigration's impact on the working class may go a long way toward explaining another big mystery when it comes to labor in America—namely, why Americans don't find unions a compelling path to the American Dream anymore.

When people in power, especially on the Left, talk about worker power, upward mobility for the American working class, and the protection of labor, they often point to unions as how you protect labor. And yet, union membership has absolutely cratered over the past fifty years. Union membership peaked in the 1950s at 30 percent of the private-sector workforce, but since the 1970s it's been in free fall—and this despite the fact that according to the U.S. Bureau of Labor Statistics, Americans who belong to unions in the U.S. make on average 17 percent more than their nonunionized brothers and sisters, with a median $1,144 in weekly earnings—compared to $958 for those not unionized.[8] It's not just wages, either. Unions offer apprenticeships and ongoing training, a debt-free career, a pension, and workplace safety and other protections. For much of the twentieth century, they were viewed as the primary vehicle for worker power and upward mobility for the working class.

Even today, approval of labor unions is the highest it's been since 1965: in 2022, 68 percent of Americans told Gallup they approved of unions.[9] It's unsurprising: Successful, public-union contract negotiations at places like John Deere and UPS have brought the power of collective bargaining back into public consciousness, and union-led efforts like the Fight for $15 normalized the idea of a $15-an-hour wage.

And yet, despite this fact, Americans aren't signing up to join unions at record rates. Just the opposite: fewer Americans than ever belong to unions, a scant 6 percent of Americans working in the private sector.[10] Many believe they are a dying institution in the U.S. There has been an uptick in unionization efforts of late, famously at some Amazon warehouses and Starbucks locations, but nothing approaching the kind of torrent that you might expect given the working conditions we're seeing. Why?

Some workers I spoke to didn't like the way that they felt unions limited their ability to rise in the workplace, with their negotiated contracts. Others had a positive view of unions but they didn't understand how they could help improve their position, or they worried a union would introduce a negative charge in their dealings with management, something they were anxious to avoid. There was also another objection that came up: Some people I spoke to viewed unions as somehow anti-meritocratic.

Skyler Adleta explained it best. He got a union plumbing apprenticeship pretty much right out of high school, but it didn't go well. His first day on the job, the journeyman supervising him told Skyler to drill twenty holes into a plywood floor. Skyler drilled the holes, which took about two hours, and then went back to the journeyman and said, "Okay, now what?"

But the journeyman was annoyed. "I told you to spend the whole day drilling holes. You spent two hours drilling holes."

"Yeah, but they're all done."

"Well, I guess then you're all done today."

"You telling me to go home?"

"I'm not. We're off at 3:30."

Skyler stood around for a while, but he's a high-energy person, so he picked up a broom and started sweeping, but then he got yelled at again.

"What are you doing?"

"I'm sweeping!" Skyler said.

"That's not your job! Your job was to drill holes and you screwed that up."

Others have blamed the fear of corporate consolidation—and corporate retaliation—for a lack of interest in unionizing. The pressures of starting a union are immense—the equivalent of trying to hold an election in a one-party state. David Rolf, founding president of Seattle-based Local 775 of the Service Employees International Union and author of *The Fight for Fifteen: The Right Wage for a Working America*, explained: "Sort of like if you were running to become the mayor, but before you were allowed to be the mayor, you had to first fight to establish that there should be a mayor at all. And then once you establish that there should be a mayor, then you find that your opponent is the only one with access to the electorate for eight hours a day, and that they've had the voter list for years and you just get it six weeks before the election. Also they have unlimited resources." Meanwhile, there are numerous stories of ugly union busting and retaliation at companies like Tesla and Amazon. But even in companies where union busting is minimal, many people don't want to go to work and have a permanently conflict-based and litigious relationship with their boss.

This isn't the explanation favored by union bosses, who view resistance to unions as a case of working-class conservatives being bamboozled by Republicans into choosing a cultural stand against their economic interests. Union leadership views the Democrats as much better for organized labor, and though they insist that they will endorse pro-labor Republicans, those endorsements are few and far between. Labor has for a century been affiliated with the Democratic Party. From 1990 to 2014, unions accounted for $1 billion of the $2 billion spent by the thirty largest federal election donors, and 97 percent of those donations went to Democrats.[11] And yet, just 26 percent of union members call themselves "liberal," as Oren Cass points out in his book *The Once and Future Worker*.[12] Thanks to the class divide in America, some major sectors of the laboring class are increasingly made up of people who find more in common with the Republican Party, at least from a social and cultural point of view. In 2020, *Bloomberg News* found that truckers, plumbers, machinists, painters, correctional officers, and maintenance employees were among the occupations most likely to donate to Trump (Biden got the lion's share of writers and authors, editors, therapists, business analysts, HR department staff, and bankers).[13] So it's not surprising that a YouGov/American Compass survey of 3,000 workers found that "excessive engagement in politics is the number one obstacle to a robust American labor movement." "Among those who said they would vote against a union, the top reason cited was union political activity, followed by member dues," the survey found. "These workers anticipate that unions will focus on politics rather than delivering concrete benefits in their workplaces, and don't want to pay the cost." Meanwhile, fear of retaliation was the least cited reason workers gave for why they haven't unionized.[14]

There is an emerging cultural disconnect between the people who most need unions and the people who more often than not run them. At the national level, union staff—especially on the political and public-policy side—are very likely to be part of what one longtime union leader called the "revolving door of Democratic operatives in Washington." They have often been guilty of subordinating core, working-class interests to what he called "the permanent culture of progressive, college-educated

SECOND CLASS

coastal elites." They are alienating the workers they're supposed to be representing, who are much more socially conservative.

Still, most workers wouldn't give up better pay just because their union boss puts their pronouns in their email signature. Eric, for example, a conservative union electrician in Pittsburgh, sees the disconnect between the guys on the job, who are extremely conservative, and the union management, who are all Democrats. "But you just don't talk about it at work," he told me. "You only talk about it with guys who share your views. My boss is extremely Democrat and I don't talk politics at work. I put that aside because I don't care. As long as he's writing my paycheck, I could [not] care less what his politics are. That's how we view it in the trades: you just don't talk about it." To Eric, the reason the trades are dying comes back to a crisis in fatherhood: Fathers aren't teaching their sons the power of unions. And in many families, there isn't a father to teach them.

But there's a much less discussed disconnect between unions and the working class, and it has to do with the way that union leadership came to embrace mass immigration in a way that directly undercut workers' economic interests.

For much of the history of labor in this country, unions were solidly in favor of limiting immigration, for all of the reasons working-class people have today: the American Federation of Labor felt that increasing the supply of labor meant giving power to employers over employees. Immigrants were often brought in as strikebreakers, which limited union power, and immigrants were willing to work for less. But organized labor did a 180-degree reversal on immigration in the second half of the twentieth century, coming to embrace immigrants, both legal and illegal, and by 2000, the president of the AFL-CIO called for amnesty for millions of undocumented immigrants. "The only way to stop the race to the bottom in wages and standards is for working people of all races, religions, and immigration status to stand together and demand an end to policies that put profits over people," reads a section on immigration at the AFL-CIO website,[15] where, unsurprisingly, in a blog post enumerating five causes of wage stagnation, immigration doesn't make the cut.[16] Yet this reversal meant advocating for a policy that many working-class Americans—of both political persuasions—view as being in direct contradiction to their economic interests.

Nowhere is the power that tough immigration policy has to improve the lives of the working class more clearly on display than in Las Vegas.

If you want to see what a real union town looks like, there's one place you have to go on pilgrimage: Las Vegas. Vegas truly is the Promised Land for service-industry workers. Whether you clean hotel rooms or bake pastries or wash dishes, if you do it in Las Vegas, you do it while earning a living wage, with full health care, a pension plan, and even help buying a house.

You can feel that the American Dream is alive and well walking through the casinos. It's in the optimism of the staff, in their swagger. There's no place in the country where service-industry workers are so fairly treated, and the quality of their service reflects the quality of their compensation. Vegas just *works*, and as a result, it's a magnet for folks looking for good jobs in the hospitality industry—jobs with dignity where they can and do spend their working lives for two or three decades before retiring.

The average pay for a union member in Las Vegas is $26 an hour including benefits. Health care is completely free for workers and their families—there are 145,000 Nevadans on the Culinary Workers Union's health-care plan—and they all have a pension, access to legal funds, job training, and up to $25,000 in payment assistance to purchase their first home. These benefits are guaranteed by the casinos in the contracts negotiated every five years by the unions, toward which workers pay $49.50 a month—voluntarily, because Nevada is a right-to-work state, meaning even people who benefit from a union contract can opt out of paying dues. But not many do—only about 5–10 percent. The union represents 60,000 guest-room attendants, cocktail and food servers, banquet servers, porters, dishwashers, kitchen workers, and laundry workers.

"Anywhere else, if you're working in a restaurant or if you're cleaning toilets or you're cleaning rooms, these are poor-people jobs," Ted Pappageorge, secretary-treasurer for the Culinary Union, told me. "And the only difference is if there's a union. And if you have a big union presence, then the nonunion has to compete, too. They gotta pay, otherwise, they can't get people. They might be able to stay nonunion, but they gotta pay."

Health care is the most important issue to the union workers. Their health care plan is a PPO, not an HMO, with no deductible and no copays. "Those are strike issues for our members," Pappageorge says. "But that takes a lot of hard work, a lot of organizing. We're a fighting union. We're a rank-and-file union." The negotiating committee is made up of 1,100 shop stewards who volunteer their time. "That's the glue that kind of holds us together." And it's ensured union members the best health care around. They are currently building centralized health centers where people can see a primary care doctor, get dental care, see a physical therapist and an optometrist.

The casinos pay $5.88 for every hour worked toward health care for workers. They pay $1.55 for every hour worked toward the pension plan. They pay seven-and-a-half cents on every hour worked for the training fund and the premier hospitality training facility. And they pay two cents for every hour worked for the housing fund, which has put more than 1,000 union members into their own homes, and provides them with legal services and financial counseling too. These benefits were all fought for over the past fifty years.

How did they do it? Can Las Vegas be a model for the rest of the country?

In a limited sense, it can be, if you think of it through the lens of something called "sectoral bargaining." Sectoral bargaining is when an industry, a region, or an occupation, sets standards for employment across the industry. The practice is very common in Europe, and it's why service-industry jobs across the board pay more there.

"The casinos are basically engaged in sectoral bargaining," Cass told me. "If some of the casinos were organized and some of the casinos weren't organized, and the ones that were organized had higher labor costs and had to charge higher hotel rates and give worse odds in their casinos, the whole thing might fall apart fairly quickly." Plus, the casinos have another huge advantage: You pretty much have to go to Vegas to gamble—there, or a few other places in the country. "Imagine if we had a law that said if you would like to drive a car, you must go to Detroit and buy one from the Chevy showroom. I'm pretty sure the Chevy workers would've done okay," Cass said.

But it's also a clue about how to scale what's working about Las Vegas outside the gambling mecca. Collective bargaining remains a crucial component of worker power. Cass recommends co-ops, sectoral bargaining, and labor cooperatives as a way of utilizing the power of the many that don't have the baggage of unions. All are common across Europe and provide avenues for workers to find power in numbers that don't involve unpopular partisan politics. One example is the Teamwork for Employees and Managers (or TEAM) Act, introduced by Florida senator Marco Rubio, which would require companies with profits of more than $1 billion to give workers a representative on the corporate board and would also allow workers to form voluntary organizations with employers "for the purpose of discussing matters of mutual interest, such as quality of work, productivity, efficiency, compensation" and more. Current federal labor law bans workers from organizing outside a formal union process, and the TEAM Act would aim to undo the ban.

But there's another aspect to Las Vegas that's a lot less replicable across the country, and it's the kind of employer you have there—a heavily regulated one with a massive profit margin that needs not only a reliable and satisfied workforce but one willing to advocate for their bosses—which the union does. It's a symbiotic relationship rather than an adversarial one; the union flexes its political muscle on behalf of the industry, lobbying Congress, for example. "I like to think we have good relationships with these companies because if the companies don't make money and they don't do well, we're not going to be able to do well," says Pappageorge of the Culinary Workers' Union.

When it comes to political organizing, the union isn't philosophically opposed to supporting Republicans, which they have in the past, but it's getting rarer. "We're not gonna support anybody that doesn't recognize the need for unions," Pappageorge says. "That's dumb. It's not in our self-interest, and it's not in the interest of workers. And it's kind of where we've ended up right now." That means organizing heavily on behalf of Democrats. "We do a lot of political work—voter registration here in Nevada, but also nationally through our parent union, Unite Here, we lobby in Congress. We move working-class people to vote that may not necessarily want to vote. They feel like they're kind of left behind."

This political muscle means that the union has something concrete to offer the casinos in addition to a strong, healthy, qualified workforce that's happy to come to work every day—something the casinos need badly. And it's the grease on the wheels of the contract negotiations. "They have to respect you, because there's no company at the end of the day that is going to just simply roll out benefits unless they respect you and they know that you're organized and you'll fight back and stand up for yourselves, and you're not a doormat," Pappageorge explained. "At the same time, we have the ability to tell these companies we will support them in their interests. If they're going in front of Congress for expansion or growth, we have the ability to support that [...]. On the gaming side of things, we've been a powerful force for these companies that if they do the right thing, then we'll back them up."

I asked Pappageorge why he thinks just 6 percent of the private sector is unionized. "There's been an assault on the idea of unions," he said. Pro-union Republicans don't exist anymore. The Labor Relations Act is weak. The biggest companies—Amazon, Walmart, and Uber—are all nonunion with no protections. "And having a union election with the National Labor Relations Board is kind of like having an election in Russia. It's on the employer's property. You gotta walk through the management to get there. They control what you can do, and they can fire you or bribe you or threaten you or whatever. And there's very little penalties."

It's why the union is so supportive of President Biden— by and large because of his championing of the PRO Act, or the Protecting the Right to Organize Act. The PRO Act seeks to amend U.S. labor laws to expand collective bargaining by preventing employers from holding mandated meetings against unions, strengthening legal protections for unionization efforts, and allowing the National Labor Relations Board to fine employers for violations. It also allows unions to collect dues from all employees at a unionized workplace, whether or not they are members of the union, weakening "Right-to-work" laws that allow workers to opt out of joining a union and paying dues, even if their workplace has a union that negotiates on their behalf.

But if anything, the success of collective bargaining in Las Vegas at securing the American Dream for service-industry workers is an argument in favor of letting workers have the choice. Workers flock to Las Vegas in order to join the Culinary Union, because they know what it has achieved on their behalf through its history and the uniqueness of its employers. The union has successfully made the case to its workers that, as Pappageorge put it, "the idea that you should be alone and somehow try to take on this economy and this world and all those forces out there that are really opposing what working people need is a way to lose." Rather than circumventing workers and using the federal government to force them to pay union dues or punish employers, the Culinary Union has done the hard work of *convincing* the casinos and their workers that it's in everyone's interests to cooperate—which it undoubtedly is.

But there's another crucial factor in protecting working-class people operating in Las Vegas that is at odds with where the Democratic Party and even the Culinary Union are at, at least rhetorically. Because the casinos are so highly regulated, they are extremely careful about only hiring people who are legally allowed to work in the United States. And this sets them apart from the service industry in every other part of the country, but especially in big Democratic cities like Los Angeles, New York, Washington, D.C., Seattle, Boston, Atlanta, and Houston, where six in ten undocumented immigrants live and presumably work.[17] Seven million immigrant workers in the United States are here illegally, making up 4 percent of the U.S. workforce, and 40 percent of them work in the service industry where they are paid less than minimum wage.[18] More than 30 percent of New York City's cooks and 54 percent of dishwashers are undocumented.[19]

With a glut of workers who will work for $5–$10 an hour, how can legal workers expect to compete, let alone make a living wage? If the casinos could hire undocumented workers and pay them a quarter of the wages they paid American workers, the whole edifice would break down.

When it comes to worker power, all the labor laws in the world wouldn't protect workers if government also supports a policy of sending jobs overseas *en masse*, or bringing in millions of workers as a permanent underclass of undocumented laborers willing to work for less money and with no protections. "Labor policy is only one mechanism of worker power," Oren Cass explained to me. "A coherent immigration policy is also a way of affecting worker power. A coherent trade policy is also a way of affecting worker power. Because if you've got a really great electoral bargaining system set up for your industry, but you're also just welcoming in stuff from China made with forced labor, then what's the union really going to be able to get? Or if you're also saying, well, employers can also just under-the-table hire illegal workers, what are you going to achieve?"[20]

In reversing their opposition to mass immigration, America's national unions ended up shooting themselves in the foot, telegraphing to desperate American workers that they will stand by the direct competition. When seen through this lens, it's less surprising that Americans aren't rushing to join unions, despite respecting the work they do to support labor.

I asked the Culinary Union's representative about whether the fact that the casinos can't hire illegal immigrants helps their workers. In response, I got an email stating the Culinary Union's position on the matter—"Culinary Union is supportive of comprehensive worker-centered immigration reform and supports a pathway for the eleven million undocumented immigrants to be able to come out of the shadows. Undocumented immigrants are already working and paying taxes in many aspects of the USA's economy and the time is now for Congress to pass immigration reform." Attached to the email was an article headlined, "America Needs Immigrants to Solve Its Labor Shortage."

Unions undoubtedly improve the lives of working-class Americans. They secure excellent health care, a living wage, workplace training and protections, and a dignified retirement. No one who stands for the working class should oppose the power of collective bargaining, and anyone who does is not serious about upward mobility or the American Dream. And yet, with just 6 percent of the private sector belonging to unions and no sign of that changing, even in this extremely pro-union environment, it's hard to see how unions truly represent the way we widen the pathway to the American Dream, though changing their tune on immigration would certainly make them more popular with the workforce that desperately needs their representation.

Even more helpful would be for politicians of both parties to abandon their elitist, self-serving commitment to mass immigration and instead listen to what workers are begging them to hear: they aren't anti-immigrant, but don't they deserve to live in a country that sees their well-being as a priority?

Limiting immigration may not solve all the problems that the working class faces in the U.S. But worker power is absolutely tied to the number of workers in the workforce relative to the number of jobs. More workers means the bosses have the power, while more jobs means the workers have the power. It's the most obvious equation of supply and demand. And yet, when it comes to immigration, everyone seems to forget this simple math.

It's never been clearer than it is now. The post-pandemic labor crunch gave workers their first gains in decades. And yet, the labor shortage was met with the worst-policed southern border, perhaps in U.S. history. The Biden administration released millions of illegal immigrants into the country, and they had the exact impact on the economy you might have expected, filling jobs and halting the gains of working-class Americans in their tracks.[21]

Simply admitting that this is happening—instead of gaslighting working-class Americans or calling them racist for seeing the impact of things like mass migration in their paychecks—is the first step to fixing the problem. The second step would a real border policy that protects American workers from the competition of millions of low-wage workers illegally entering the country. The third step would be an immigration policy that, instead of catering to corporations, prioritized the well-being of the working class. Limiting the supply of workers who compete with the working class will have a huge, direct impact on the quality of their jobs, because their bosses will have to work harder to keep them. This is the most direct way of protecting the American worker and improving the lives of the working class. Forcing companies to verify the legal status of their workers and eliminating guest-worker programs will go a long way toward penalizing companies for screwing over American workers, and will force them to make the jobs they need done into good jobs that provide American workers with a shot at the American Dream.

CHAPTER 6

THE BENEFITS CLIFF

When I met Kevin Nelson, he and Kevin Harper were in business together. Kevin N. is tall and thin with black hair, world weary, soulful eyes and an accommodating hunch for those shorter than him, which is everyone. Kevin Harper is shorter, bald, and fills out his shirt and tie like a man who means business. He has a neat goatee, and his penetrating eyes seem constantly on the move, squinting in skepticism or humor by turns. He was the perfect counterbalance to Kevin N., who had started a janitorial services company, Quality Cleaning Solutions, during the pandemic, and had asked his old friend from the army Kevin H. to come on board and help with the administrative side of the business. Both Kevins come from hardscrabble backgrounds, in Compton and Long Beach, and both enlisted in the military right out of high school. When we sat down to talk in a nondescript municipal building in Riverside, California, they spoke with one voice about matters of business. But there was one topic that they disagreed on, and it was the role of government benefits.

Kevin Harper falls much more on the personal responsibility side of things. "I'm not political," he told me. "And I don't want to offend too many people that, as we say, are *of the culture*," he said, making air quotes with his fingers. "There he goes, already did it, it's too late!" He laughed at himself. "But I look at it like, hey, get out there, and even if you don't want to be an entrepreneur, there's a job out there that you can go ahead and try to apply for, try to get, if you want to work. People that want to work will find work, even the people that have, say, those issues where they were in prison. I see those people; they're driving around the neighborhood with trucks doing salvage. They find a way to make it happen until they can make it happen. But then there are other people sitting around like, 'Hey, I'm not gonna move unless it's for the right dollar.' But you don't have anything! If I was at home and I had nothing, absolutely nothing, and I had to depend on my wife or my mom or whoever to take care of me as a man—especially as a man—I would think, 'What do I need to do to change my situation?' and I would go start the process. So it's hard for me to fathom why do people not think in a fashion that's productive, instead of wanting to receive."

"I'm a little bit more liberal about some things than he is," Kevin N. stepped in. "I can be a little bit easy sometimes on people when it comes to being able to do certain things."

"Out of all people, he's the one that should *not* feel that way," Kevin H. interrupted. "You shouldn't expect anybody to come save you. There is no savior. But he wants to still feel like other people in bad situations just need help," Kevin H. said.

"Well—" Kevin N. tried to interrupt, but his partner wouldn't let him.

"You did the most to make sure that you got out of that situation," Kevin H. insisted. "I'm not saying we're not special. I'm special, he's special, everybody's special. But everybody has the ability to look at themselves, take accountability, get out there, and work hard, man! If it's not working for you, pivot. Figure something else out. Maybe I'm trying to work this cashier job and I can't count. It's not working out for me. I'm not learning how to count any day soon. Maybe I go try this construction job over here. Oh wait, they didn't wanna let me in because I'm kind of weak. I'm fragile. I could either work out and get strong enough for the job, or I could maybe go paint."

"His expectation is high," Kevin N. said. "I tell him, we're *this*," he said, holding his hand above his head parallel to the floor. "And not everybody is."

"You gotta fight," Kevin H. said. "It's your life, you gotta fight for it. If you don't, if you don't do that, who do you expect to try to help you more than yourself? You know the game is unfair, but you have to play it anyway."

"See, I tell him, I know what he went through when we first got in the military," Kevin N. replied. "I watched them try to break him, literally try to break him, and he's a little guy, you know, short guy. And I watched as they tried to break him in every way that you could break somebody. He didn't break. And I tell him all the time, you don't realize you're the cream of the crop. You're here," he held his hand up high again. "Not everybody is there. Some people it's gonna take time to build. Some people may never be there, but you are *here*. But this is why we are here in this moment—because we're leaders. We were built for this position. Now let's take this and let's go."

The debate between the Kevins over how generous government benefits should be is one that's happening in working-class homes across the country. There is deep ambivalence toward government assistance programs. On the one hand, many working-class Americans know intimately the pinch of poverty, and many have people in their families and communities who are part of the dependent poor due to disability or addiction or stints in prison or who are single mothers, who rely on government services, and for whom they would be financially responsible without those programs. But they also know people they feel could be working, yet have chosen not to and instead rely on welfare entitlements— entitlements that they pay for with the taxes that come out of their often too-meager paychecks. There is a feeling of injustice—that the people who truly need and deserve benefits can't access them, and that fraud is rampant. The feeling of unfairness and often-firsthand knowledge of welfare fraudsters makes lower-income people hesitant to support expanding welfare—because it would end up costing more without any guarantee that the right people would reap the benefits.

Even Kevin N.'s "liberal" view of the government helping people didn't look anything like what you might hear from progressives calling for expanding welfare. "I don't necessarily have a problem with paying into the system to help as far as Medicaid, Medicare, food stamps, or social-service systems, because the one thing I do know, you never know in life when you might need some help or need these social-service systems," he told me. But when I asked him if he thought expanding the social safety net would help working-class people, he was unequivocal.

"No. I think opportunity helps," he said. "To me, the welfare system is broken in a sense, because you can give people a small amount of money, food and all that, but those are Band-Aids for their situation; it's not a cure for their situation."

"What would a cure look like?" I asked.

"You have to give opportunities. That's the biggest thing if you want people to get out of the system: the opportunities have to be there to get out of the system. Welfare doesn't help you off the system. It's just a crutch. And it kind of keeps you dependent on the system. Opportunities—that's the biggest thing."

The idea that more government benefits may help some people but it will ultimately create more dependence was something I heard a lot. Nicole, the Ohio DoorDasher, said the same thing Kevin did when I asked her if she thought we should raise taxes on corporations and the rich to fund a more robust welfare state.

"I have mixed feelings with that idea," Nicole told me. "To some degree, it would help, but would it really fix the problem? The problem falls back to opportunity for us in poverty. The more the government hands out to us in poverty, the less chance we have to get out of poverty and get an opportunity to make our own way and our own American Dream. People get very comfortable with government assistance, and they relax on trying and making an actual effort to rise above the poverty level. If large corporations are going to require college degrees, a higher tax bracket for the wealthy should fund education for us to have opportunity instead of handouts."

The view that the government is funding the wrong things is extremely common in the working class—even those who are more on the Left. "Unless a person is physically or mentally disabled and unable to work, housing and SNAP benefits should only be temporary for people to transition from hard times to stable times through either job placement or college or trade training programs," Cyrus, the Phoenix-based former hazmat trucker, told me. "Tax the rich and corporations to fund the social services the majority of Americans want. The majority want universal K–trade school, universal health care, and a baseline wage that allows a single mom to buy a simple house for her and her kid. In a functioning democracy, the people *get* what they want, regardless of what you or I think. If you look at all the universal policies Americans want, we're a really bighearted people. What I oppose is using taxes to fund 'welfare' programs that subsidize slave wages codified by corporate lobbyists."

The people I spoke to didn't feel they were owed the fruits of another person's labor—even a very rich one—but they did feel that corporations made decisions to create wealth for shareholders instead of workers. Where they supported redistribution, it was for purposes of upward mobility. What they wanted was an economy that shared the wealth with the people who created it, and a government that helped people get a leg up when times were hard.

Instead, I heard again and again that the government penalized work, giving money to people who chose not to work. They sometimes ended up with even more money than people who worked extremely hard and then, because of that work, became ineligible for assistance when they needed a little help getting by.

The lowest-income people I interviewed frequently brought up something called "the benefits cliff," the phenomenon where if you make too much money, or get married to someone who's earning more than you, you lose access to crucial benefits like government health insurance that are not guaranteed by even some good-paying jobs. The benefits cliff creates a perverse incentive for people to decline raises or better jobs because the benefits are not just worse than those of the government, but in some cases totally inadequate or even nonexistent.

For example, the National Conference of State Legislators (see fig. 10) calculated that when a single parent with one child in preschool and one child in school gets a raise from $8 an hour to $12 an hour, she loses her SNAP benefits. When she gets a raise from $15 an hour to $15.50, she loses her child-care subsidies, which amounts to a cost to her of more than $7,000 a year in the best-case scenario, or 25 percent of her yearly income, despite just making $0.50 more an hour. It will take a raise from $15 an hour to $24 an hour just to recover what she lost when she got that extra $0.50.

Figure 10. The Benefits Cliff Measured as the Loss of Benefits Relative to Increase in Wages for a Single Parent With Two Children.

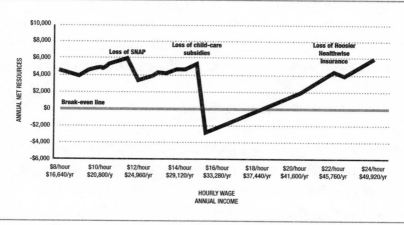

The National Center for Children in Poverty's Family Resource Simulator, published by the National Conference of State Legislators.

Clearly, the benefits cliff majorly disincentivizes making small advances at work, such as accepting more hours and better pay. No rational person would or should give up 25 percent of their resources, especially when it comes to their children.

It also disincentivizes marriage in the working class—which can be a stabilizing force in an uncertain world—not just emotionally, but economically. Researchers have long pointed out that married people earn more than those who aren't married, by as much as 30 percent.[1] Married men on average make $80,000 a year—compared to just $50,000 for their non-married counterparts. And this is across racial groups.[2] While the racial gap persists across the board, married Black men outearn single white men and single white women. The median income for married heads of Black households is more than $90,000—compared to just $38,000 for their unmarried counterparts. The poverty rate for Black Americans in 2020 was nearly 20 percent—but for Black married couples, it was just 6 percent. And there's a massive trickle-down impact on their kids: children raised by two parents do better than children raised in any other family structure, so much so that a state's share of married parents is the best predictor for upward mobility for poor kids—better even than race or a college education.[3]

Why do married families make so much more money? Some economists believe that men who make more money are also more attractive to women as partners, making them more likely to get married. Others believe the opposite: the personality traits that make men good workers are the same ones that make them good husbands. Others argue that married people pool their incomes so they can save more, while still other economists think that married men work harder, or that married people can take bigger risks in looking for better jobs because they can rely on their partner's income if things don't work out.

One thing is for certain: divorce can make you much poorer. There are lawyers, court costs, the cost of a second home, the cost of shuttling the kids back and forth, and childcare now that both parties have to work. Fathers have to pay child support, which often comes out of their salaries in substantial ways.

Yet, despite the benefits of marriage and the cost of divorce, marriage rates have fallen dramatically for working-class Americans in recent decades. Back in 1960, whether or not you had a college degree had no impact on whether you were likely to be married. Seventy percent of Americans twenty-five and older were married, regardless of how educated they were. By 2015, a huge gap had emerged: 65 percent of bachelor's-degree holders were married, compared to just 50 percent of people without a college degree.[4] Meanwhile, single parenthood skyrocketed for those without a college education. One-in-four children are now born to a single parent, but just 13 percent of babies born to college-educated women are born out of wedlock.[5] And yet, instead of incentivizing marriage, which would help many of these families, the government makes it prohibitive, because for poor working-class moms, it often means making a big sacrifice and giving up life-saving government benefits that they would lose if they got married.

"Right now, a lot of our policies targeting the poor end up basically bringing poor people almost level with working-class folks without the benefit of working full-time or being married," says Brad Wilcox, director of the National Marriage Project and professor of sociology at the University of Virginia. Meanwhile, people who did everything right are penalized.

People living on the edge of poverty are often faced with a choice of not getting married or lying. Cyrus, the Phoenix trucker, has married and divorced Nona, his wife of decades, not once but twice—once to wipe her credit clean so she could get an FHA housing loan, and a second time so she'd qualify for Obamacare. Almost no one Cyrus knows who's married is actually married. It's just too prohibitive.

Amber and David Lapp have devoted their lives to answering the question of why working-class Americans are getting married less and less, given the host of benefits the institution offers. In 2010, Amber and David were newlyweds a year out of college living in New York City. Amber was teaching and David was working for the Institute for American Values, a think tank focused on the family, when his boss asked him if he knew anyone who wanted to go to the Midwest and interview white working-class people about how they think about marriage. David came home to Amber and said, "Hey Amber, do we know anybody that would want to go to the Midwest and talk to working-class people about how they think about marriage?" And Amber said, "We want to do that!" So they moved back to Amber's hometown, South Lebanon, Ohio, and started knocking on doors and talking to people, asking them about marriage and how they were forming families. They were so moved by people's stories and the feeling that they had found where they were meant to be that they moved to the working-class Ohio neighborhood where they were doing the interviews the following summer. They've been there ever since, and have kept in touch with many of the families they interviewed over the course of the decade.

The most striking thing they found in their initial 2010 study was that the main reason people didn't get married was deep-seated trust issues. The people they encountered very much *wanted* to get married, and had a deep reverence for the institution, but they also expressed a reluctance to make a binding vow for fear that they were not with the right people. Many had seen their parents cycle through multiple partners and failed marriages, and when they talked about their own futures, they talked a lot about how they really didn't want to get divorced. These strong anti-divorce attitudes were in many cases keeping them from getting married. People told Amber and David that they revered marriage, and because they did, they had to be careful because marriage can cause problems if it's to the wrong person. You need to make sure that you're completely set before you get married, because otherwise the weight and pressure will send you to divorce. And divorce is the last thing you want because of the experiences they'd already had with it as kids.

An easy first step to eliminate the government tax on marriage would be to make the child tax credit available to married couples and to immediately double the threshold for Medicaid so that married couples don't lose their coverage. It would put an end to the harmful mentality that's so focused on helping the poor that it ends up unintentionally penalizing those who have been making all the right choices and playing by the rules, but wind up getting left behind. In a series of focus groups in Ohio and Georgia and Texas, working-class Black Americans repeatedly brought up this mentality to Brad Wilcox and his fellow researchers, and their frustration that working full-time did not give them much of a return on investment compared to their friends who were poor or not working and getting all these benefits from the government.

The link between financial stability and marriage has been called the "success sequence" by researchers in an attempt to brand a formula to help young adults succeed. The formula has three steps: Get a high-school diploma, work full-time, and get married before having kids. For a sample of nearly 9,000 millennials who followed this sequence, researchers found that 97 percent of them weren't poor by the time they became adults, while 52 percent who missed all three steps were still in poverty.[6]

And yet, I was surprised when my own research did not find such a neat picture. Granted, my sample size was much smaller than 9,000. But among the people I met in my year traveling the country, I met many who had had children before getting married who were living the American Dream—people like Patrick, the NYPD detective, or Kevin Harper, whose wife had a child when they got married, or Jim, the bartender. There were a lot of blended families and a lot of women who had found a lifelong partner of thirty years after multiple failed marriages that had yielded children, and still made it to the middle class. I also met a lot of people who were married that worked every day of their lives and were dead broke—people like Corrie and Nicole and Lucia. Maybe they wouldn't qualify as "poor," but they certainly wouldn't call themselves a success story. That doesn't mean people didn't think marriage was important. Men especially brought it up as something they cherished and needed to become who they were meant to be and without which they would be living much less stable, satisfying lives.

Another thing that surprised me was how working-class people thought about health care. People didn't talk about health care like other entitlements. They didn't see it in the same category as food stamps or childcare or housing assistance. Many people I spoke to believe it should be guaranteed by the government. I was surprised to find how many of the conservative working-class Americans I interviewed supported something like universal health care, Medicare for All, or at least a government-backed catastrophic plan. Almost everyone qualified their opinion by saying they didn't know enough about the subject, or that they weren't sure how we would pay for it, but the ballooning costs of health care in this country and the idea that people's health had become part of a capitalist system where someone was making a profit was abhorrent to many people. Even those who opposed a government option did so because they had no trust in the government to pull it off or that it would not abuse the power.

Skyler, the Ohio electrician, considers himself a conservative, but when I asked if he would support universal health care, he said something I've never heard a conservative politician say. "I'd say, in principle I would, but I don't know enough about policy or the economic machinations around UHC proposals to make me believe it could be a sustainable reality. I think that social security being so horribly mismanaged is an indicator that our government may not be the most responsible structure to uphold something like universal health care. If gambling away citizens' retirement is a minor offense (which it isn't, it is detestable), then the idea of our government gambling away lifesaving health care because of mismanagement is a major one. To be honest, I'd love to see a viable option for it. I just don't have faith that our government would be able provide it or uphold it without sacrificing quality and consistency."

Kevin Harper, who is deeply suspicious of government assistance, had a similar response when I asked if he thought there should be a single payer, say, Medicare for all Americans. "That's a good question," he told me. "I think it's a good thing, but I don't know the repercussions of everybody having health care. I don't know how that would affect the industry. But as a human with good intentions, I think that everybody should be able to get seen if you're sick. You should not be dying outside because you couldn't make money."

He got no disagreement from his friend Kevin Nelson there. "I need some dental work done, and I haven't been able to do it because of the expenses," he told me. "I just think everybody should be able to have health care. It is just so much money being made, you know? We have to do a better job of that. We have to find a way to take care of people. We live in a society where people want to make money, and everything is a moneymaking machine. And people find a way to take something as delicate as health and turn it into profit-making. So then you have a lot of people who suffer in life, who die early because they couldn't afford to take care of themselves. And I think that is sad—very sad and unfortunate."

Amy, the Florida CNA, also pushes off going to the doctor, because she has a $3,500 deductible, which means that nothing is covered until that is met. I asked if she supported universal health care; she saw both sides of the issue, as she did all issues. "I've heard that if we do that, the cost is going to go up," she said. She didn't think it was a bad idea for the government to have an option, but she wondered if the answer wasn't for corporations to give better benefits to the employees who create all their profit. "I kind of think that if you work for a company and they're a billion-dollar company, why can't they come up with better health insurance for the employees?" She said. "I think we should maybe hold these companies a little more accountable for the employees that they hire, give them better benefits that way. And that actually would retain your employees a lot longer as well."

"The medical-insurance-hospital-industrial complex needs a major overhaul," Gord, the Ithaca-based truck driver, told me. "It clearly costs way too much money." But Gord is more ambivalent about a single, government-backed health insurance, having experienced one growing up—both its strengths and limitations. "One of the things about growing up in Canada is that we are constantly bombarded by propaganda—they're constantly comparing themselves to the United States, and the number one point of comparison is, 'Those heathens down south don't have national health care. What kind of supreme moral failing for such a rich country!' But then if you need some kind of specialized cancer treatment in Canada, you can get on a list for eight months, but you might be dead before you get it. When you grow up underneath that thing, and then you travel the world and see how the rest of it operates, it disabuses you of certain notions very quickly, at least if you're paying attention." There are pluses and minuses to a single-payer system, Gord points out. "In Canada, you get in an accident, you break your leg, you go to the hospital, they'll fix you up. But if you need to see a specialist for anything, or you want do something that's a little bit outside the normal procedures of established medical protocol, you're either gonna be waiting for months or it's just not gonna happen."

Like Gord, others I spoke to had their concerns about government-backed health care. Jamie, the Home Depot manager, was opposed to it on the grounds that it would give the government too much control over people if they also controlled their health insurance. And Jim, the Brooklyn bartender, worried about who would cover the bill to insure everyone. But, by and large, I found a lot of consensus on this issue. People felt that health care should not be a for-profit industry, and they couldn't understand why their taxpayer dollars went toward providing excellent health care for politicians while they themselves couldn't afford to go to the dentist. They couldn't understand why the richest country on earth has a workforce made up of people like them who work and work and work, and yet no one seems to think that their health matters—not the government they support, nor the companies they create profit for.

"It's as simple as, I'm paying for Joe Biden's health care. I'm paying for his crackhead son's rehabilitation. I'm paying for all that. I want what I'm paying for. That's it. We want what we're paying for," Cyrus, the truck driver from Phoenix, told me. "I think the most viable way to do that right now is a public option that allows any American to buy into the same subsidized system that their Democrat and Republican politicians are already getting. Whether it's Marjorie Taylor Greene or AOC, whichever your flavor. They both have access to the same health care." At the end of the day, policy should reflect what people want, and what they want is high-quality affordable health care. "The majority of Americans want universal health care," Cyrus told me. "And in a democracy, theoretically, the majority should get what they want."

CHAPTER 7

HOUSING

Nicole grew up in poverty. "We were very lower class," she told me sitting at a park near the home she rents in South Lebanon, Ohio. "I knew I was poor, but my parents always made sure I had food and clothes. My mom sewed a lot—she made my clothes." She stayed home with Nicole while her dad worked. He laid carpet floors and worked on the Cincinnati River boats. He did that for forty-eight years, and only stopped at seventy-seven. He never had much by way of savings, and they now get by on social security, which nets them $1,500 a month. And yet, despite all this, they were able to buy the home Nicole grew up in, and while the property taxes keep going up, which is quickly becoming a problem for them on their fixed income, the home they were able to buy when Nicole was just nine months old provides them with a little bit of stability.

But Nicole herself doesn't see how she will ever be able to buy a home. She lives on an even tighter shoestring, bringing in $1,300 a month driving for DoorDash and babysitting and cleaning homes. She pays $1,000 in rent, which leaves just $300 for food and utilities, which almost always exceeds that. She's paying 75 percent of her income in rent, and makes $20 a month too much to qualify for Section 8. She wouldn't qualify for an FHA loan because she doesn't have enough credit built; she always avoided credit cards because they seemed really dangerous. And she doesn't have anywhere near enough money for a down payment.

"Do you think Section 8 should be available to people who make just a little bit more money, like you?" I asked.

She paused for a minute before answering. "I do," she said. "But at the same time, there's so many people that take advantage of it. It's such a fine line." She paused again. "I'm gonna be honest with you: When we DoorDash, we DoorDash a lot to HUD housing, Section 8, and things like that, and they got brand new cars in the driveway. And that for me that is like . . . well, there's a fine line."

Carlos Padilla is in better shape than Nicole, but he, too, despairs at his chances of being a homeowner. He's worked as a pastry baker at the Las Vegas hotel and casino Treasure Island for the past twenty-nine years. He came to Las Vegas from Flagstaff, Arizona, where neither of his parents had graduated from high school; Carlos's father worked as a welder for the city, and his mother worked two jobs—she was a line cook in two different restaurants. But, unlike Carlos, they own their own home.

"When I first moved here, I wanted to come live the Las Vegas dream," Carlos told me. "And I started building on that, and now I feel like I'm being knocked down, you know? The American Dream right now is hard to grab, and I want to be able to grab it."

When Carlos first moved to Vegas, the word was that working on the strip was the job to get. He got hired as a pastry chef and started immediately as an apprentice. They trained him on the job, and a year later, he was a full-blown baker. Over the course of his thirty years, his pay rose from $15 an hour to $25 an hour. His bosses encouraged him to keep up his education, too. He took classes in sugar and being a chocolatier. He learned how to make breads and pastries and cannoli and tiramisu with rum—that's his specialty. During the slower months, from November through December, his executive chef encourages him and his colleagues to experiment with their own recipes. His mom started calling him from Flagstaff, getting him jobs, calling him on the regular and saying, "Can you come over next weekend and make this cake?" She'd get the cake started, and he'd drive the four hours out to Flagstaff and finish it off.

Carlos met his wife at the Culinary Union. He's a shop steward, and she was a fellow union organizer from Brooklyn who worked at the Mirage at the time as a guest-room attendant, a job she eventually left to become a schoolteacher. But they are struggling to achieve the American Dream. Carlos's landlord has raised his rent by $600 in the last couple of years, and it just keeps going up. He's worried he won't be able to afford to live in Las Vegas if this keeps up. With the price of food these days, his phone bill, and rent, there's not much left over to save from the $49,000 a year Carlos brings in, even with what his wife makes.

It's a story I heard again and again: Even working-class Americans who make enough money to cover their bills can't find a foothold when it comes to the housing market.

How do we solve this problem? How do we get these costs down?

On the Right, there tends to be skepticism about fixing the housing problem in urban centers at all. Instead, conservatives advocate for picking up and moving.[1] Meanwhile, on the Left, the answer is simple: have the government pay for it. When it comes to housing specifically, there are calls for building more affordable housing, expanding Section 8 and public housing, and just generally growing the safety net to house more Americans who have fallen on hard times. Representative Maxine Waters of California, for example, is seeking $150 billion for "fair and affordable housing investments" and for expanding Section 8.[2] President Biden's behemoth spending bill, Build Back Better, included a host of provisions for housing, from investments in public housing, to rental assistance, to down payment assistance.[3] The plan included $15 billion to build or preserve 150,000 rental homes for low-income families. There is a YIMBY movement that advocates for more affordable, subsidized housing, and now advocates have begun to discuss the idea of "universal rental assistance."[4] Others still have called for a vacancy tax on empty homes, or for a ban on private equity buying property.

These all sound like good ideas for helping low-income Americans who are struggling to pay for housing. And yet, none of them provide a pathway to the American Dream; in fact, what you'd see as a result is the opposite: a glut of Section 8 housing vouchers would instantly jack up the price of housing in any place experiencing a shortage, because there are suddenly many more people who can afford the same tiny number of available units.

When it comes to housing, free housing provided by the government is not only not politically feasible, it's not a pathway to the American Dream. And it doesn't jibe with the desires of working-class Americans, who don't want to live at the beneficence of government but want a fair shot at making it on their own and providing for their families with dignity.

"It's not the government's business to be subsidizing housing," Cyrus, the Phoenix truck driver, told me. "The free market works." The problem is that workers aren't being paid the real cost of their labor, which should be pegged to what it costs for them to live in dignity. "If you had a baseline wage that was pegged so that a single person could rent an apartment where it was 30 percent of their income, you wouldn't need a subsidy for housing."

Cyrus himself managed to buy a home once. He saved up $10,000 working 100-hour weeks for $14 an hour in the Halliburton oilfields while living with his wife Nona in a travel trailer in a windswept trailer park in Salt Lake. He took that money and bought a house for $125,000 in Phoenix and moved down there to do local trucking. That's when the economy crashed in 2008, and suddenly his house was worth $25,000. "Obama took my house," Cyrus recalls bitterly. The bank refused to renegotiate the mortgage, which infuriated Cyrus because they had enough money to bail out the banks, but not enough to renegotiate mortgages? So like many, many other Americans hit in 2008, Cyrus walked away from the house, which destroyed his credit. So the couple came up with another plan: they got officially divorced, Nona declared bankruptcy, and then went back to her maiden name. When she applied as a first-time homebuyer for an FHA loan, the bankruptcy didn't show up on her credit report, and they were able to buy another home in Phoenix, where they still live.

For Cyrus, the problem is not one of supply but of demand: people just aren't paid enough to afford housing. Somehow, we've accepted a system in which millions of Americans work for wages that don't actually cover the cost of living. In other words, the true cost of their labor—to go to a job so you can have a roof over your head—is being either borne by workers or the government through subsidies, but not by the corporations that employ workers, who are getting off paying a fraction of that cost.

The problem is there is also a huge supply crunch. The housing market itself is an absolute disaster. We are currently short somewhere between five million and six million homes in the U.S. In six states across the country, housing costs seven times what the average person makes a year. Those same states are riddled with enormous homeless populations.

How did we get here? For Edward Pinto, a senior fellow and director of the Housing Center at the American Enterprise Institute (AEI), the problem can be summed up in one word: zoning. Pinto has spent his entire career in housing. He was the chief credit officer for Fannie Mae until the 1980s and worked in affordable housing before joining AEI. So he's spent his life trying to get middle- and lower-income Americans into their own homes. And what he's learned is that whenever the government gets involved in housing, it makes things worse and makes housing more expensive.

Back in 1914, John Nolan, a famous urban planner, did a study called "A Good Home for Every Wage Earner." He did a survey of what was being built back in 1914. And he found a lot of what Pinto calls "light-touch density"—duplexes and townhouses and three-story homes called triple-deckers that were manageable for working families to buy and start building equity. But two years after Nolan's study came out, an attempt to secure equity of a different kind would tragically get in the way of what had been a common way for working-class Americans to become homeowners.

In 1916, the Supreme Court ruled that you couldn't use race in zoning policy because it violated the Fourteenth Amendment. What that meant was that urban planners would have to find another way to keep Black Americans and other people they considered racially inferior—southern and eastern European immigrants, for example—out of new neighborhoods, since they couldn't use zoning laws to do it anymore. Around the same time, Herbert Hoover authorized a zoning commission, whose members also took it upon themselves to find some way to keep those undesirables out of new neighborhoods that circumvented the Supreme Court's ruling. They figured that if they couldn't zone Blacks out, they would price them out. The urban planners realized that if they could make the housing a bit more expensive, it would be out of the reach of Blacks and immigrants because they would never make enough to buy into those neighborhoods.

Enter the single-family detached housing zone. Hoover's committee created a recommendation that outlawed anything but single-family detached homes in neighborhoods that otherwise would have been full of duplexes and triple-deckers interspersed between single-family detached homes, which would have resulted in Americans of all income brackets and races living side by side. Instead, the federal government put out a model-zoning ordinance that specified limiting significant tracts of land to single-family homes, and then the government strongly encouraged states to adopt the ordinance, which virtually all states did. Along with single-family detached homes came things like minimum lot sizes, side yards, and backyards—a growing list of things these families needed.

By the end of the 1920s, exclusionary zoning had taken over the United States, with 52 percent of urban areas implementing zoning restrictions. As a result, big parts of the country were devoted to the kinds of homes that today only the rich can afford.

Exclusionary zoning was quickly followed by the practice of redlining, in which the government only backed mortgage loans in certain neighborhoods, further widening the divide between those who could afford a home and who couldn't. In 1934, the Roosevelt administration established the Federal Housing Administration, a mortgage-insurance program, as part of the New Deal to help get Depression-era construction workers back to work and turn America from a nation of renters into a nation of homeowners. But the FHA was explicit in its 1935 *Underwriting Handbook* about where it would and would not back mortgages, and it discouraged banks from lending to buyers in or anywhere near racially integrated neighborhoods and schools on the specious grounds of ensuring "neighborhood stability." "If a neighborhood is to retain stability it is necessary that properties shall continue to be occupied by the same social and racial classes," the handbook warned, producing maps that portrayed "high-risk" neighborhoods in red—hence redlining. As a result, the white suburban housing market flourished, helping middle-class Americans begin to ascend into the upper classes, while excluding poor minority and working-class families from the benefits of what would turn out to be a huge government investment.

Redlining didn't just target Black Americans; there were plenty of people we would consider white today who were redlined out of desirable neighborhoods with government-backed, single-family detached homes on the grounds of social class, economic or educational achievement, or where they came from. But with enough time and money, some immigrants could overcome these barriers, which was impossible for Black Americans and the poorest whites. These racial covenants were outlawed by the Supreme Court in 1948, but by then, the advantage given to those Americans lucky enough to qualify for those single-family detached homes had turned from privilege into entitlement, and they found a way to solidify their status and seclusion on their own—without the help of government—with the NIMBY movement.

The "Not in My Backyard" movement was born in San Francisco in 1956, when high-status hotels banded together to convince the local zoning board that areas zoned for hotels must exclude lower-status motels. Watching this unfold, property owners realized they had a newfound power: they could attend zoning hearings, delay things, demand hearings, sue and make their voices heard, which is exactly what they proceeded to do. It took a while, but the NIMBY movement caught on like wildfire across California and by the 1970s, housing prices there began to separate away from the national median and absolutely explode. The movement spread up the coast, then made its way to New York and Boston, which outlawed the triple-deckers—those three-story, three-family homes that were a common and affordable way for working-class families to become homeowners.

That's how we got to today's housing market. The housing shortage is a direct result of zoning: 78 percent of the land in the United States that is zoned as residential land is zoned for single-family detached homes.

Some of this has to do with the two-income household. Once upon a time, doctors married nurses and lawyers married secretaries. Today, highly credentialed elites tend to marry each other, and they tend to live in big cities where they command big salaries. Everyone else is now competing for a dwindling stock of homes against power couples that have not just two incomes but two incomes in the top 20 percent. While you might have expected couples to keep the second income for emergencies, the logic of supply and demand doesn't have a carve out for savings accounts; the second income of those professional couples was simply absorbed into the price of housing where they live, quickly making homes twice as expensive.

This was the central insight of Massachusetts senator Elizabeth Warren and her daughter Amelia Warren Tyagi in *The Two-Income Trap: Why Middle-Class Parents Are Going Broke.* "If two-income families had saved the second paycheck, they would have built a different kind of safety net—the kind that comes from having plenty of money in the bank," writes Warren. But families didn't save the money—because they *couldn't* save the money. "Instead, families were swept up in a bidding war, competing furiously with one another for their most important possession: a house in a decent school district. As confidence in the school system crumbled, the bidding war for family housing intensified, and parents soon found themselves bidding up the price for other opportunities for their kids, such as a slot in a decent preschool or admission to a good college. Mom's extra income fit in perfectly, coming at just the right time to give each family extra ammunition to compete in the bidding wars—and to drive the prices even higher for the things they all wanted."[5]

Warren recommended reregulating consumer lending and limiting interest rates to halt the rise in foreclosures and "take the ammunition out of the middle-class bidding war." Yet, none of that would help the simple problem of supply and demand. There just aren't enough houses—period. And there isn't enough housing because of zoning laws. Any government initiative that helps on the *demand* side—by securing more families thirty-year mortgages, say, or Section 8 vouchers, or building affordable housing initiatives, end up hurting the situation, because they increase *demand* without increasing *supply*, making housing even *less* affordable.

"The market could provide plenty of housing if the public policy would only allow it to be built," explains Pinto. What's needed is very simple: Take an ax to zoning laws and allow duplexes back into those neighborhoods. Bring back light-touch density and you will solve the housing shortage in a decade.

How? By Pinto's model, if you implemented light-touch density in the areas with the most potential for it—coastal metro areas—allowing for three or four or five units on parcels of land currently zoned for single-family detached homes, you could add nine million units over the course of ten years, and another nine million in the following ten years. Pinto estimates you'd get 900,000 new units a year for the next thirty to forty years.

"Light-touch density is also naturally inclusionary," says Pinto. "Why is it naturally inclusionary? Well, the incomes of individuals don't have to be as high. Some of the units are going to get rented. Some of the units are going to be owned. There's going to be just a real mix. You get much more variety both in terms of incomes, in terms of ethnic origin, in terms of renter versus owner. From a supply side, that's the way that in my mind, you get more homeownership and more resilient homeownership."

It would also help with the homelessness crisis. Pinto and his colleagues at American Enterprise Institute created a map of the country in which you can see the hallmarks of the NIMBY movement on either coast, where instead of a home costing two or three times an average worker's salary, it costs more than seven times that. And it's in those parts of the country where the rate of homelessness is absolutely skyrocketing. In California, for example, a home costs on average seven times the median income. California is also home to 30 percent of America's homeless population—though it is home to just 12 percent of the overall U.S. population.

Pinto found that the places where the ratio of median home price to median total income was high, where people were paying more than four times their income to buy a home, were also the places where the homeless rates were highest. He gave it a name: the displacement rate.

Displacement can take on many different forms. You might move in with your parents, or some friends, or you might move into your car. But the longer you're displaced, the more chance there is that you're going to run into an issue. And if you end up on the street, the longer you're there, the more difficult it is to get back onto the ladder. The thing is, if you live in an area with low displacement pressure—where the median home price is just three times the median annual income—you probably won't be displaced for very long, even if you lose your home, because there's a lot of housing to go around. You're probably going to be able to get back on the ladder. But if you live in a place where there is a dire shortage of housing, and you just fell off the ladder, the likelihood that you'll be able to quickly find a place is much lower.

One thing Pinto found is that while New York and Los Angeles have higher wages, the increase for working-class Americans is not enough to compensate for the higher housing prices. For example, a truck driver in the New York City area makes a median annual wage of $37,000 but with a median monthly rent of $1,300, he's paying 43 percent of his wages on rent. In Los Angeles, the median wage is only $36,000 a year, while the median rent is $1,500, meaning he's paying over 50 percent of his wages on rent. Meanwhile, in Albuquerque, New Mexico, the median pay for a trucker is $33,000 a year, but the median rent is just $690 a month, meaning he's only paying 24 percent of his wages on rent. In Houston, it's 32 percent. In Akron, Ohio, it's 28 percent.[6]

Or take construction workers: Their median annual wage in New York is $50,000 a year, which means they pay about 30 percent of their income for housing with a median one-bedroom apartment going for $1,300 a month. In Los Angeles, on the other hand, their median annual wage is just $42,000 a year, meaning they are spending 44 percent of their wages on housing. Compare that to Billings, Montana, where the annual wage is similar to LA—$41,000 a year—but the median rent for a one-bedroom is just $602, meaning construction workers in Billings are only paying 17 percent of their wages toward rent.[7]

Or take another example: The median wage for a person who works in food prep in the New York City area is $29,000 a year. In Los Angeles, it's $27,000 a year. In Kansas City, it's just $22,000 a year, and in Louisville, Kentucky, it's $21,000 a year. But if you compare it to the median rent, those who work in food prep in Kansas City are only paying 33 percent of their wages to rent, as opposed to those working in Los Angeles, who are paying $1,500. That's a whopping 71 *percent of their income*. This is the kind of person who gets squeezed out, displaced to their parents, then their car, then the streets.

The Salvation Army estimates that 62 percent of the homeless people they service were recently housed. That's an astonishing statistic.

The good news is, fixing this problem is easy. The better news is, creating stability at the bottom also creates upward mobility. The bad news is, there are a lot of people suggesting things that don't work at all.

"I started in affordable housing almost fifty years ago," says Pinto. "Affordable housing does not work. It's way too expensive. We don't have enough money, even with the printing press that we have, we do not have enough money. We've been doing this for fifty years. We've wasted trillions of dollars on this stuff over the years. We did all that public housing stuff, tore most of it down. They're now converting motels at $400,000 a bed into an efficiency unit. Somebody's making money there, but it's not really helping the homeless. You can't build enough subsidized housing in California because as you build subsidized housing, it creates more demand. Think about it: If you were to give a voucher to everyone with an income below 80 percent of the median income right now, a quarter of people with incomes below 80 percent get a voucher. If you gave it to 100 percent as an entitlement, rents would soar. People who are sharing an apartment voluntarily, why would you share an apartment if you each got a voucher? You'd be creating new demand."

The only answer is to tackle the supply side and create more housing—much more housing, by getting rid of zoning laws so the market can naturally create light-touch density housing.

The good news is, six states have already passed light-touch density bills in a desperate bid to not become the next California. Montana, whose displacement index hit 5.1 recently, just passed a bill this year, as did Vermont, Washington State, Oregon, and even California. And Florida and New York are starting to talk about it. That means of the six states with the biggest housing problem, four have new light-touch density bills and the two remaining are starting to consider it. "We have the wind at our backs," says Pinto. The main impediment to the American Dream is rich liberals. But while rich liberals are not likely to abandon their NIMBYism, their kids are much more conscious of the issue and much less likely to keep others from the privileges they enjoy.

Pinto and his colleagues at American Enterprise Institute found that the most potential is actually where the highest cost of housing is. There's huge opportunity in New Jersey, Massachusetts, Philadelphia, and Washington, D.C., where the price of a home is the highest in the country.

Unlike many conservatives, Pinto is not suggesting that in order to be housed, working-class Americans need to move to rural areas and abandon their families and communities and jobs. Nor is he suggesting the government give people free housing. Instead, Pinto is saying that the local governments where American workers live can easily meet them where they are at by allowing the free market to do its thing and create more supply to meet the varying levels of demand.

It's the solution that most jibes with how the working-class people I spoke to talk about their own needs, with a focus on self-sufficiency and the government getting out of the way rather than intervening. Instead, government should even the playing field so the system isn't rigged against them in favor of the rich.

I ran Pinto's solution by many of the people I talked to while writing this book, and they all thought it sounded like a good idea.

"I think it's interesting and viable," Gord said. "I'm imagining that the pushback against this by, as you say, liberals is probably a certain type of county or neighborhood where they have their land and they don't want it to look like the cities they live in, which is very convenient. But if people can build a home and then have another unit either built right into it or some kind of other situation where you could rent part of that out and build up your equity, that's all fine and good. I support that 100 percent."

I posed the idea to Amy, the CNA from Florida, and asked if she would personally be interested in a duplex as a starter home.

"Yeah, sure, I don't think it's a bad idea at all. Anything that will help. But can I ask you, what stops them from rezoning it?" Amy asked.

"Wealthy couples in expensive neighborhoods who don't want the zoning to go away because if it's zoned for single-family detached, that means that their homes go up and up in value," I said.

"You know what, I kind of thought that's just about something you were gonna say," Amy said and laughed. "I call that greed. I do understand their point: I would want to get as much as I could out of my house. But there's also a point of you have people that have nowhere to live."

CONCLUSION

When I first decided to write this book, I wanted to know if working-class Americans still had a fair shot at the American Dream. To answer that question, I spent a year traveling the country and asking working-class people what they thought about it. I asked them how they defined the American Dream, whether they thought they had been given a fair shot at it, and if not, what would help them get there. I asked them which political party they thought was better at fighting for the American Dream, and what their political views were. I asked them how much money they made and what they spent it on, and what their personal lives were like, and what their families were like growing up. I asked deeply personal questions and I met people who were not only willing to answer them but eager to have their voices heard.

Throughout the course of that year, things changed, and for many of the people I interviewed, there were small improvements to their lives. Nicole was able to find a set of affordable dentures. Nehemiah left McDonald's and got work as an orderly at a hospital where the starting salary is $15 an hour. But for others, things also got worse. Kevin Harper and Kevin Nelson's partnership fell apart. Corrie found part-time work but no home and is now considering splitting up her family, leaving one child with her sister in the hopes that she'd have more luck finding a smaller apartment. Gord lost his job trucking and had to take up construction work. But mostly, things stayed as they were, and the American Dream remained elusive for floating and struggling working-class Americans. This was true even for many who felt they had made all the "right" decisions, people who worked extremely hard yet couldn't get a foothold in the middle class.

And despite the radical diversity of the working class, there was a surprising consensus in the things that would help. Higher wages. Housing. Better health care. Fewer migrants competing for their jobs. Trade policy that favored America. Overall, good, high-paying jobs that rewarded their immense efforts with the kind of modest rewards that so many in the top income brackets take for granted: A home. A vacation with their kids now and again. Good health care. Enough in the bank that they don't have to call the electric company every month to beg forbearance to keep the lights on. Some money put away for retirement when their aching bones can no longer do physical work.

Of course, the working class is not a monolith. A group of people as radically diverse as America's working class is bound to have a lot of diversity of opinion. And yet, there was a lot less diversity on questions of politics and policy than I had been expecting. Working-class Americans are keenly aware that more unites them as Americans than divides them.

By and large, I met a lot of people who said they would never consider getting an abortion yet felt appalled at the idea of an abortion ban. Most people supported a moratorium on immigration, both legal and illegal, for the foreseeable future, but also supported a government-backed catastrophic health-care plan or even full health-care coverage. People were very pro-gay but very worried about transgender ideology. They supported taxing corporations and the rich, but not expanding the welfare state. There was a lot of frustration about people they felt chose to live off the government and not work—but also anger at corporations that maximized profit at the expense of their workers, and politicians who didn't care.

This set of views characterized most people I spoke to, as it does most Americans. And yet, neither political party represents these positions. One party supports taxing corporations and expanding health care, but also allows teenagers to medically transition, and expands welfare and much more immigration. The other party wants to restrict immigration and limit welfare, but supports corporations and lowering taxes on the rich, and its representatives never utter the word "health care" except as a slur.

Who should the working-class vote for? In the best-case scenario, they can pick one party that supports half of their views but actively undermines the rest. It's at best a crapshoot, which explains the working-class frustration with both political parties.

It also explains why working-class Americans aren't polarized. Polarization in this country is an elite phenomenon. Political and media elites tend to agree with the vast majority of the party platform they vote on, believing that the party to which they devote their spiritual energy has chosen wisely on unrelated topics like immigration, climate change, and abortion. But working-class people know that the unique set of policy proposals each party has chosen is arbitrary, so they have enormous forbearance for working-class people who pick the other party. The way they vote only reflects a portion of their political views, and extremely little of their larger identities. You can't be bound to a party that only represents half of your views, and actively undermines the other half. And you can't hate someone for choosing the other one when it's such a crapshoot.

The truth is that we have one party in this country that represents corporations and the Chamber of Commerce and another that represents the educated, credentialed elite and the dependent poor, and no party willing to assume a working-class agenda, which is why the American Dream is out of reach for so many. Republicans rail against wokeness while protecting corporate greed, while Democrats push for more welfare while welcoming millions of migrant workers. Both have abandoned the working class whose labor we all rely on to survive.

This situation is untenable—morally, spiritually, and economically. No society can survive that's built on the labor of those with no voice.

Yet a surprising amount of energy is expended keeping the working class silent. When two thirds of working-class white Americans voted for Donald Trump, they were dismissed by the elites as deplorables. When they tried to speak up against COVID lockdowns and vaccine mandates, they were smeared as grandma killers and fascists. When they tried to point out that mass immigration was hurting their children's futures, they were called racists. When they continued to support Donald Trump in the 2024 GOP primary, they were derided for ascribing to a "grievance culture."

The elites will find any number of slurs to avoid acknowledging the truth: the American economy rewards them to a far greater degree than the people whose irreplaceable labor they rely on to survive.

Progressives on the Left like to demand that billionaires "pay their fair share," yet they are unwilling to share any of the prosperity that has come their way when we made a college degree the gatekeeper of a middle-class life. Meanwhile, conservatives on the Right demand that the working class—the GOP's new base—sacrifice their one vote on the altar of fighting wokeness, while elites in the party revert to the free-market policies that have impoverished their voters.

It's disgusting—and unsustainable. You can't have a democracy where the majority of voters have no party to vote for that represents their interests. Something has to give.

Politicians should stop running against the interests of the American people and take a page out of the working-class playbook. More unites us as a country than divides us. Anyone telling you otherwise is trying to use you to make money and consolidate power. Hate fuels elite power and pocketbooks. Luckily, it's easier to see through when the proceeds are landing in someone else's bank account.

For the working class, *this* is the Promised Land. Yet we've relegated them to the status of second-class citizens. This cannot stand. We need to revive the American Dream. The future of this country, and the future of our democracy, depend on it.

ACKNOWLEDGMENTS

I will never be able to express the gratitude I feel for the people who opened their lives to me, who trusted me to tell their stories in this book. I called them again and again, asking personal and invasive questions on every topic under the sun. They were endlessly generous with their time and their thoughts and their lives. I feel so truly humbled by this trust, and I hope this book reflects the truths they entrusted me to tell. This book is dedicated to them.

Thank you to Joe Price, Katherine Wilson, and Megan McQueen at Brigham Young University who helped me convey the quantitative picture of the American working class, and to Gavin J. Hamrick for helping me with research for this project. My thanks to Brad Wilcox and Nick Wolfinger, whose research helped me understand the subject. Thank you to Goldie Goldbloom for help with editing. Thank you to Amber and David Lapp: you are a model to everyone working in this space about how to do it with respect and love. Thank you to Oren Cass at American Compass for laying the policy groundwork for a better tomorrow and for generously funding this project.

Thank you Renata Bystritsky, Seth Mandel, Bethany Mandel, Adaam James Levin Areddy, Ilana Teitelbaum, and Melanie Notkin—for the delight of your friendship and for reading this material first. You each made this book so much better.

Thank you to Nancy Cooper, Philip Jeffrey, Ramsen Shamon, and Jason Fields for being incredible colleagues while I worked on this project. I am so deeply honored to work with you all at *Newsweek*. I still can't quite believe my luck.

Thank you to my agent Don Fehr for the constant guidance, and to the whole team at Encounter Books. Thank you—especially thank you—to Roger Kimball, who bet on me once again.

And thank you as always to my Zo.

NOTES

PREFACE

1 Anne Case and Angus Deaton, "The Great Divide: Education, Despair, and Death," *Annual Review of Economics* 14 (2022): 1-21.

INTRODUCTION TO PART 1

1 Mark J. Perry, "Manufacturing's Declining Share of GDP Is Inevitable, Global, and Something to Celebrate," AEI Ideas, American Enterprise Institute, March 22, 2012.

2 Abby Budiman, "Key Findings about U.S. Immigrants," Pew Research Center, August 20, 2020.

3 Hillary Hoffover and Andry Kiersz, "Home Values Have More Than Doubled in the US Since 1970," *Business Insider*, December 18, 2018.

4 Ibid.

5 American Compass Family Affordability Survey. This book was supported by a grant from American Compass.

6 Stephen J. Rose, *Social Stratification in the United States* (New York: The New Press, 2020), 12.

7 Ibid., 14.

8 American Enterprise Institute, "Restoring Opportunity for the Working Class," November 27, 2018.

9 Case and Deaton, "The Great Divide: Education, Despair, and Death."

10 David Leonhardt and Stuart A. Thompson, "How Working-Class Life Is Killing Americans, in Charts," *New York Times*, March 6, 2020.

11 Case and Deaton, "The Great Divide: Education, Despair, and Death."

12 Odeta Kushi, "Why Educated Millennials Still Hold the Key to Future Homeownership Demand," *First American*, October 10, 2022.

13 2022 U.S. Trends Report: Landmark Changes in Americans' Financial Health; Financial Health Pulse.

14 American Community Survey, 2020.

15 Ibid.

16 Data compiled for me from the American Community Survey by Joe Price *et al.*

CHAPTER 1: STRUGGLING

1 U.S. Government Accountability Office, "Federal Social Safety Net Programs: Millions of Full-Time Workers Rely on Federal Health Care and Food Assistance Programs," GAO-21-45, October 19, 2020.

2 Edward Rodrigue and Richard V. Reeves, "Five Bleak Facts on Black Opportunity," Brookings Institution, January 15, 2015.

CHAPTER 3: RISING

1 American Compass, "Family Affordability Survey," February 14, 2023.

2 Sharon O'Malley, "Which Occupations in Construction Have the Highest Rate of Homeownership?" Construction Dive, October 21, 2014.

3 U.S. Bureau of Labor Statistics, Occupational Employment and Wages, May 2022: 47-2111, Electricians, www.bls.gov/oes/current/oes472111.htm.

CHAPTER 4: GOOD JOBS

1 Obama White House Archives, October 25, 2013.

2 Interview with Oren Cass.

3 Joseph B. Fuller and Majari Raman, "Dismissed by Degrees: How Degree Inflation Is Undermining U.S. Competititveness and Hurting America's Middle Class," Accenture, Grads for Life, Harvard Business School, October, 2017.

4 Oren Cass, "The Workforce-Training Grant: A New Bridge from High School to Career," Manhattan Institute, July 16, 2019.

5 David H. Autor, David Dorn, and Gordon H. Hanson, "The China Shock: Learning from Labor-Market Adjustment to Large Changes in Trade," *Annual Review of Economics* 8 (October 2016): 205–40.

6 Adam Dean and Simeon Kimmel, "Free Trade and Opioid Overdose Death in the United States," SSM Population Health, August 2019.

7 Justin R. Pierce and Peter K. Schlott, "Trade Liberalization and Mortality: Evidence from U.S. Counties," *American Economic Review: Insights* 2 no. 1 (March 2020): 47–64.

8 "Domestic Steel Manufacturing: Overview and Prospects," Congressional Research Service, May 17, 2022.

CHAPTER 5: WHOSE JOBS?

1 Statement of Peter Kirsanow to the Senate Subcommittee on Immigration, March 16, 2016.

2 "Immigration Raids Yield Jobs for Legal Workers," *ABC News*, September 13, 2009.

3 Statement of Peter Kirsanow to the Senate Subcommittee on Immigration, March 16, 2016.

4 Budiman, "Key Findings about U.S. Immigrants"; Federal Reserve Economic Data, "Shares of Gross Domestic Income: Compensation of Employees, Paid: Wage and Salary Accruals," October 26, 2023; Charles Hugh Smith, "Why Wage Inflation Will Accelerate," Swiss National Bank, May 15, 2021.

5 Oren Cass, "Jobs Americans Would Do," American Compass, May 4, 2023.

6 Ibid.

7 Ibid.

8 Bureau of Labor Statistics, Union Members Summary, January 19, 2023.

9 Megan Brenan, "Approval of Labor Unions at Highest Point Since 1965," *Gallup News*, September 2, 2021.

10 Bureau of Labor Statistics, Union Members Summary, January 19, 2023.

11 *The Once and Future Worker* (New York: Encounter Books, 2018), 143.

12 Ibid., 144.

13 Jackie Gu, "The Employees Who Gave Most to Trump and Biden," *Bloomberg News*, November 2, 2020.

14 American Compass, "Not What They Bargained For: Worker Attitudes about Organized Labor in America," September 2021.

15 AFL-CIO, Issues: Immigration, https://aflcio.org/issues/immigration.

16 Kenneth Quinnell, "Five Causes of Wage Stagnation in the United States," AFL-CIO, January 15, 2015.

17 Jeffrey S. Passel and D'Vera Cohn, "Twenty Metro Areas Are Home to Six-in-Ten Unauthorized Immigrants in U.S.," Pew Research Center, March 11, 2019.

18 Budiman, "Key Findings about US Immigrants"; Annie Nova, "Feast or Famine: How the City's Restaurants Would Collapse without Undocumented Workers," Invisibile Hands.

19 Ibid.

20 Interview with Oren Cass for this book.

21 Jeanna Smialek, "A Flood of New Workers Has Made the Fed's Job Less Painful. Can It Persist?" *New York Times*, July 24, 2023.

CHAPTER 6: THE BENEFITS CLIFF

1 Scotty Hendricks, "Married People Earn More Than Single Individuals. Here's Why," Big Think, January 5, 2022.

2 Quentin Fottrell, "Married Men Earn More Than Everyone Else (Including Married Women and Single Men," Market Watch, November 19, 2019; Ana Hernández Kent and Lowell R. Ricketts, "Wealth Gaps between White, Black and Hispanic Families in 2019." Federal Reserve Bank of St. Louis, January 5, 2021.

3 W. Bradford Wilcox, Robert I. Lerman, and Joseph Price, "Mobility and Money in U.S. States: The Marriage Effect," Brookings Institution, December 7, 2015.

4 Kim Parker and Renee Stepler, "As U.S. Marriage Rate Hovers at 50%, Educational Gap in Marital Status Widens," Pew Research Center, September 14, 2017.

5 "The American Family Today," Pew Research Center, December 17, 2015.

6 W. Bradford Wilcox and Wendy Wang, "The Power of the Success Sequence," American Enterprise Institute, May 26, 2022.

CHAPTER 7: HOUSING

1 Carmel Richardson, "It's Not a Housing Shortage," *The American Conservative,* September 23, 2022.

2 Debra Kamin, "Maxine Waters Proposes Billions to Expand Low-Income Housing," *New York Times,* June 21, 2023.

3 Taylor Locke, "Build Back Better Includes $170 Billion for Affordable Housing," *CNBC News,* November 24, 2021.

4 Janaki Chadha, "Study: Expansion of Federal Rental Assistance Would Bring Significant Drop in Poverty, Homelessness," *Politico,* September 20, 2021.

5 Elizabeth Warren and Amelia Warren Tyagi, *The Two-Income Trap: Why Middle Class Parents Are Going Broke* (New York: Basic Books 2016), 12.

6 American Enterprise Institute Housing Center's Good Neighbors Toolkit.

7 Ibid.

INDEX